WHAT THE BIBLE SAYS ABOUT GOD'S RELATIONSHIP WITH BLACK PEOPLE

Henry L. Razor

S.H.E. PUBLISHING, LLC

Biblically Black & Blessed
Copyright © 2021 by Henry L. Razor.

All rights reserved. Printed in the United States of America. No part of this booklet may be used or reproduced in any manner whatsoever without written permission except in the case of brief quotations embodied in critical articles or reviews.

For information contact :
www.shepublishingllc.com
info@shepublishingllc.com

Book Cover & Title Page Design by Michelle Phillips of CHELLD3 3D VISUALIZATION AND DESIGN

ISBN: 978-1-953163-31-8

Revised Edition : January 2022

10 9 8 7 6 5 4 3 2 1

THIS BOOK IS DEDICATED to the memory of all of the saints at the Earle Church of God in Christ that raised me in the Gospel. The names are far too numerous to name them all. Nearly all have transitioned to heaven, but their memory lives on with me.

TABLE OF CONTENTS

Introduction i

In The Very Beginning 1

The Garden of Eden 12

The Black Adam and Eve of the Bible 27

Black People – The Descendants of Ham Through Cush 36

Black People are God's People 61

Notable Black People of The Bible 97

Black People Restored 118

Acknowledgements

First, I give thanks to God for His direction and guidance while preparing this work for distribution. When I had questions, you answered them, when I didn't quite get it, you explained it to me, when I needed confirmation, you directed me to the right places at the right times. You continue to show yourself great, and for this, I am grateful.

To my wife, Janette, who was very patient with me during this project, I say, 'Honey, I thank you so much.

To my daughter-in-law, Larita, who project managed this book from start to finish. You are one in a million, and your commitment to success and perfection is unmatched.

I must acknowledge my graphics artists, Michelle Hudson and Michelle Phillips, for their brilliant work designing the covers, and Kendra Wiley, whose tireless work to provide the illustrations when requested in a short time saved this project.

And to the entire Faith Hope & Charity Church family, many of you have requested of me to write this book for years. I thank God for such a loving church.

Pastor Henry Lee Razor

Are ye not as children of the Ethiopians unto me,
O children of Israel? saith the LORD…

> Amos 9:7 KJV

Introduction

WE ALL KNOW that February is Black History Month in America. This celebration of the history and contributions of black people was started in 1926 by black historian and scholar Carter G. Woodson.

At Faith Hope & Charity Ministries, we remain true to the original intent, mission, and purpose of Dr. Woodson for February by using it as a time of education, focus, and teaching about the assignment of God to black people and God's relationship to/with black people overall.

This book is **not** intended to malign, denigrate, disparage, vilify, bad-mouth, or speak evil of any ethnic group, nationality, or people. But rather, this book emanated and sprang forth from the teachings of Pastor Henry L. Razor during Black History Month. These teachings identify, highlight, and focus on the assignment and responsibility that God has placed with the indigenous Africans or black people. It is an assignment that is often dismissed, overlooked, or ignored by many that use the Bible as a guide for living, yet this assignment is critical to the plan of God for all of the earth.

BIBLICALLY BLACK & BLESSED

Far too often, when the biblical record of the descendants of Ham, indigenous black Africans, or black people is presented, it is embellished, then presented from a position of hate by those whose purpose and goal is to utilize hate for their ungodly purposes. The very fact that their presentation is from a position of hate makes it ungodly because God is love. This book uses the Holy Scriptures to show God's assignment and purpose for all people, regardless of race, ethnicity, or national origin. When this assignment is known, respect for each other is realized, love can abound, and harmonious living is the result.

When the role of black people in the Bible and in God's plan is understood as clearly as the role of the Shemites (who are descendants of Shem), and the Gentiles (who are descendants of Japheth), our relationship with God is strengthened and our ability to accomplish His purpose and will in the earth is energized. So the goal of this book is that after reading it, researching it within the context of a Biblical structure, and praying, you will have a clear understanding of God's assignment and purpose for black people, and this acquired knowledge will strengthen your relationship with God and all humanity. God's assignment to black people demonstrates God's desire that all men live synchronously and in harmony while fulfilling His plan for humanity on the earth.

I currently serve as Senior Pastor of Faith Hope & Charity Ministries in Chicago, Illinois. The intent and purpose of my Black History Month teachings are to highlight the rich spiritual heritage of black people while identifying and celebrating the long-standing relationship that black people enjoy with God.

It is crucial that black people understand and know their assignment from God and celebrate their rich spiritual heritage. This is important not only for black people, but all people should know and understand this heritage, not only in February but also every day of every month each year. This book aims to provide insight into God's relationship with all mankind, specifically bringing into focus God's purpose, plan, and relationship with black people and how this relationship impacts the world.

In my life, I have observed many things of many people of different cultures. I was educated and trained as an electronics engineer. As an engineering manager, I have enjoyed the opportunity of developing relationships with, associating with, and managing a multi-culturally diverse team of technical engineers. During my professional technology career, I managed engineers in thirteen countries on five of the seven continents. I was fortunate to have the opportunity to closely observe individuals from diverse cultures; individuals who practiced different religions; individuals who had various belief systems.

In my observations, it always stood out to me how spiritually aware black people are. Whether African Americans, Native Africans, Briton Nationals, or those of African heritage relocated to other regions of the world, the singular most prevalent commonality that I noticed was their spiritual awareness. I know that this is a very unscientific observation. Still, it was apparent that black people are the most spiritually aware, God sensitive, Supreme Being seeking people on the face of the earth. This book also provides biblical explanation, reasoning, and substantiation for my observation.

Indeed, all mankind can benefit from understanding God's purpose and relationship with black people. Understanding God's relationship with black people provides a foundation for God's expectation, mission, and purpose for everyone. All races and ethnic groups are prominent in God's universal plan for the redemption of this world, and no people should be ignored or overlooked when exploring God's universal plan.

Therefore, I reiterate that this book is by no means intended to be anti-any ethnic group or race. But instead, the focus, mission, and purpose of this book are to highlight the universal assignment to black people made by God.

God's relationship with black people is essential to all people. This relationship should be understood, realized, and taught to everyone so that we may all know and understanding God's divine purpose for mankind.

Although much meditation, prayer, research, study, and thought went into the writing of this book, it is written with biblical references that are easily checked and researched by the reader. The intent is that this will be an easily readable and understandable expository that will be the basis for further study, as well as a reference for today's Christians. After reading this book, my hope is that black people who are God-sensitive everywhere will acquire and share a sense of Godly pride and recognition of our Godly call and purpose as black people. I also hope that non-blacks will read this to understand that it is not purposed to be anti-ethnic group or race, but rather pro-bible and pro-God. Everyone benefits when God's purpose and plans are known, implemented and adhered to.

HENRY L. RAZOR

As you read this book, I pray that you acquire an appreciation for God's purpose, not only for black people but for all people. My hope is that if you are of African heritage, this book will instill a Godly pride that will move you closer to God and motivate you to fulfill God's purpose as a people and personally for your life. If you are of non-African heritage, my hope is that you will acquire an appreciation for God's purpose and plan for black people and gain a better understanding of how God's relationship with black people impacts His relationship with all people.

BIBLICALLY BLACK & BLESSED

In The Very Beginning

> "*I*n the beginning God created the heaven and the earth." [i]

When read as it is written, this scripture appears to be a very simple and self-explanatory sentence. But if you take time and explore this, you will find that this particular verse and the succeeding verses provide insight into much more than revealed by this simple sentence. The word beginning[ii] means "the point at which something begins or starts." Have you ever asked yourself 'What was started?" or "Who was started?" Since God is doing the creating, we know with certainty that this was not His beginning. The bible has exclaimed that God has no beginning or end.[iii] Rather, this scripture references the time in which The Creator, God, started something by creating 'the heaven and the earth'.

This verse must be examined because in this verse, along with the succeeding verses, we find that God arranged the earth, organized the atmosphere, and created every living, breathing, and moving terrestrial creature known unto man today. Every living thing known today has its beginning in these verses. So, in Genesis 1:1, God starts the earth. In Genesis 1:2, we learn that "And the earth was without form, and void; and darkness was upon the face of the deep." From a child this has always puzzled me because later in that first chapter of Genesis, we see that everything else that God created was perfect at the time of creation[iv]. There was not a single time that God arranged, fixed, organized, or repaired anything that He created. Once He created anything, He moved on to the next creation so that at the end of the sixth day, everything created was perfect and complete. So then, why would the earth not be created perfect? Would God create it void and without form, and darkness all over it, thereby creating the need for it to be arranged, organized, and placed in an orderly fashion later? (*I say this if indeed this is the way it was at creation*) Or was Genesis 1:1 stating that God initially created 'the heaven and the earth' perfect, but Genesis 1:2 is referring to the rearrangement and reorganization of the earth after some catastrophic event? Let's take a look.

Throughout the first chapter of Genesis, we see the creation of everything known and understood to terrestrial man. Then in the second chapter of Genesis, we find God elaborating on His creation of Man. It is in this second chapter we are introduced to the Garden of Eden, given reference markers signifying where this garden was located[v] (*we will re-visit this shortly*), and given detail on the formation of woman. However, in the third chapter of Genesis, we find that one of God's created beings is no longer 'very good' as it was at creation. It is in Genesis chapter 3 that we first gain knowledge of the Devil. We see here that the Devil has entered into, possessed, and aligned himself with the 'serpent', and now the serpent has come under the influence of and is carrying out Satan's work. The serpent has become so closely aligned with Satan that the very word 'serpent' became synonymous with 'The Devil'.[vi] But wait! In the first chapter of Genesis, when God created everything else, there is no mention of the creation of angels! There is also no mention of the creation of the Devil! Since there is no mention of God creating the Angels or Satan in Genesis chapter 1, these celestial beings must have already been in existence as He arranged, organized, and ordered the earth. He performed all of the creation that is detailed in chapter one. This brings us back to the very first verse of the very first chapter of the very first book of the bible. This brings us back to Genesis 1:1.

Since <u>only</u> God is Alpha and Omega, the first and the last, the beginning and the end, we can say with assurance that the angels were created. And since the Omnipotent God is identified as the creator[vii], we can also say that these beings were created by God. But when were they created? And as I have previously stated, there is no mention of the creation of angels or Satan in the first chapter of Genesis. Satan shows up in the third chapter of Genesis with no record of his creation in the first or second chapters. Let's dig deeper into scripture.

Satan was once a resident of heaven. But he got kicked out or expelled from his heavenly residence. Jesus said, "I beheld Satan as lightning fall from heaven".[viii] Although he still has access to heaven[ix], he no longer has a residence there. He has been permanently barred from a heavenly address. But when did this happen? We clearly see that he had already been evicted when he first appears in the third chapter of Genesis. Let's look to the fourteenth chapter of Isaiah for an answer to this question and insight.

Isaiah 14:12-17 (KJV)

[12] How art thou fallen from heaven, O Lucifer, son of the morning! how art thou cut down to the ground, which didst weaken the nations!

[13] For thou hast said in thine heart, I will ascend into heaven, I will exalt my throne above the stars of God: I will sit also upon the mount of the congregation, in the sides of the north:

¹⁴ I will ascend above the heights of the clouds; I will be like the most High.

¹⁵ Yet thou shalt be brought down to hell, to the sides of the pit.

¹⁶ They that see thee shall narrowly look upon thee, and consider thee, saying, is this the man that made the earth to tremble, that did shake kingdoms;

¹⁷ That made the world as a wilderness, and destroyed the cities thereof; that opened not the house of his prisoners?

The very first point requiring explanation is the term 'Lucifer'. The term "Lucifer" was taken by the King James Version translators from Jerome's Latin Vulgate (383-405 A.D.) edition of the Bible. The Hebrew word is Heylel', which suggests the idea of "shining," or "bearing light." Jerome assumed the word was the name of the morning star, hence, he rendered it by the Latin title "Lucifer."

As biblical understanding increased and it was realized that Isaiah 14 contained a description of Satan's original fall, the term Lucifer came to be applied to the devil prior to his fall from grace, and this designation is commonly employed today.[x]

I start my explanation on these verses by emphatically stating that we hold that these verses in Isaiah chapter 14 are insight and detail into the eviction of Lucifer/Satan from heaven. There are numerous points of reference within scripture that supplies enough auxiliary support for this position.[xi]

So here in Isaiah 14:12-17 we see that Lucifer (Satan) decides to exalt himself and exercise rule over God, who created him. We then see that God forcibly casts him out of Heaven. (Keep in mind that Jesus said He saw Satan as lightning fall from heaven.) But what is of note for this book is the state of the created earth once Satan is evicted from heaven. Verses 16 & 17 states that Satan "made the earth to tremble", he "did shake kingdoms", he "made the world as a wilderness", and "destroyed the cities thereof". In other words, Satan's eviction from heaven made the earth '**void and without form**'.

So when God created the heaven and the earth, it was also perfect just as all of His creations are perfect. Satan's fall wreaked havoc upon this perfect creation, thus creating the need for God **to re-arrange**, **re-organize**, and **re-order** the earth. God did this in Genesis 1:3-19. This also takes us to a disagreement that many Christians have with science. Many Christians justify their belief that the earth is approximately ten thousand (10,000) years old by referring to the biblical and historical account of the ascent of man from Adam to the present. Whereas, most scientists agree that the earth is actually millions, if not billions of years older than the biblical creation of Adam.

Let me take a moment and emphasize this point. There is no need for Christians to be at odds with science in this area. As a matter of fact, there is no reason for informed and learned Christians to ever be at odds with science. Science validates the existence of God by verifying the undeniable and unexplainable works of His hands. So instead of fighting science, we can use it to prove without doubt that our God is supreme.

Although I too believe that the Adamic lineage and historical record provides the accurate and adequate age of man, there is enough bible support to show that the age of the earth and the age of man are not the same. As stated earlier, in the first chapter of Genesis God is re-organizing the earth after Satan's fall. Science has proved that the earth was in existence for millions, or even billions, of years prior to this[xii]. So although man dates back approximately 10,000 years, the earth dates back much further.

This too creates another point of contention that many Christians have with science. If the earth dates back billions of years, but man only dates back thousands of years, what or who inhabited the earth in the time prior to the creation of Adam?

In Genesis 1, we see that "in the beginning, God created the heaven and the earth". Then the very next verse we read is that the earth was void and without form and darkness covered it. So there is a time period between the first verse of Genesis chapter 1 and the second verse of Genesis chapter 1. And if Adam dates back approximately 10,000 years and the earth dates back 4-5 billion years, then that time period between Genesis 1:1 and Genesis 1:2 spans billions of years.

Now, when considering the age of modern man, there is a valid disagreement with science. Most scientists calculate the age of modern man at about 200,000 years and the age of our early human ancestors at 4-6 million years[xiii]. They arrive at these numbers by applying scientific methods to unearthed fossils. It is with this account of man's age that I, as a Christian disagree. I don't disagree with the age of the fossils, for they have been tested and consistent methods have been applied that reveal an age of 4-6 million years. I too believe that these creatures existed and lived millions of years ago, but my disagreement is whether these creatures can be characterized as 'man'.

The bible teaches that man is tripartite[xiv] and created in God's own image[xv]. So man has a physical body created from the dust of the earth. God then placed a spirit within man. This He did by breathing into him. It is this spirit that brings the body to life. Once the physical body housed a spirit, the bible says that man became a living soul[xvi]. It is the soul of man that separates him from all creation and places him in an entirely new dimension. It is the soul that makes us the image of God. It is the soul that allows man to exist in an entirely new realm. A realm that is not inhabited by any other created terrestrial beings. A realm that is a little lower than the heavenly angels, but higher than any other earthly created beings, thus allowing us to reign over the other created beings even when we are not physically larger, stronger, faster, etc. then they[xvii]. Adam was the first and only creature for which God gave a soul. Simply put, Adam was the very first '***Living Soul***' thus making him the very first man. There is no disagreement that these other creatures for which fossils have been unearthed existed. These creatures may have contained some characteristics, features, and traits of man, but they lacked the defining feature that makes a creature a man; they lacked a soul. These creatures would have existed prior to Adam, but after the time that God created the heaven and the earth. They would have inhabited the earth during a time that Lucifer resided in his heavenly residence. They would have roamed the earth with other creatures such as dinosaurs and Behemoth[xviii], and when Satan was evicted from heaven, the earth trembled, kingdoms were shaken, cities were destroyed, and the world became without form and void, or in other words, a wilderness. One result of Satan's eviction from heaven was the annihilation of these creatures, and like all the other creatures that were in existence on earth at that time, they became extinct.

MAN

CREATURE

It is with this as a backdrop that God said "Let us make man in our image, after our likeness". Then God commanded man to 'replenish the earth'[xix]. Replenish simply means populate the earth again. It is obvious with this command that the earth was inhabited prior to God re-organizing it in Genesis 1. And I will show that it was also at this time that God created the indigenous black man and initiated a relationship with him that created a portal for the entry of every human of every ethnic race into this world.

The Garden of Eden

"*A*nd the Lord God planted a garden eastward in Eden; and there he put the man whom he had formed." [xx].

With this statement, we shall begin the exploration of dark-skinned or black people. At the time of this statement, only two humans existed, and they existed in the region from which God formed them from the dust. We see from this verse that God planted a garden, which we will refer to as 'The Garden of Eden', and placed the very first man and woman in it. Therefore, if we can locate the garden, we will learn a lot about the heritage of the first man because we will have located the land to which he was indigenous, the land that produced him from the dust, the land to which he was a native.

Locating the Garden of Eden today is a daunting task at best. It is doubtful that the geographical topology of the region is the same today as it was approximately 10,000 years ago. Since the creation of the garden, the earth has experienced cataclysmic events such as the great flood of Noah's day. There have been earthquakes and other seismic events that could eliminate landmasses and re-direct rivers and waterways; the earth has also experienced natural erosion and land re-positioning inherent where water and land meet. But we are given specific geographical markers that we can use along with documented historical accounts to, at a very minimum, arrive at the region for which The Garden of Eden was located.

We know that a river flowed out of the Garden of Eden, and it split off into four separate rivers. We are also given the names of the four rivers. Two of the four rivers are yet in existence today, and even if there have been geographical topology changes in the area, they would yet be flowing in their original geographical regions. Therefore, they will provide valuable insight into the location of the Garden of Eden, and hence, the native land of the first man.

Genesis 2:10-13 (KJV)

[10] And a river went out of Eden to water the garden; and from thence it was parted, and became into four heads.

¹¹ The name of the first is Pison: that is it which compasseth the whole land of Havilah, where there is gold;

¹² And the gold of that land is good: there is bdellium and the onyx stone.

¹³ And the name of the second river is Gihon: the same is it that compasseth the whole land of Ethiopia.

¹⁴ And the name of the third river is Hiddekel: that is it which goeth toward the east of Assyria. And the fourth river is Euphrates.

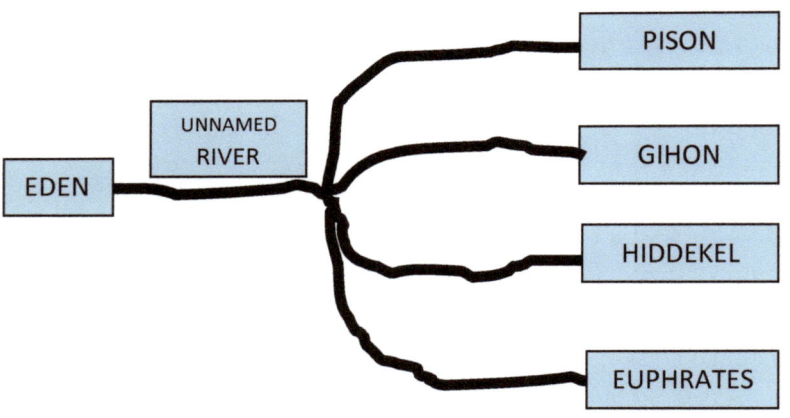

FIVE RIVERS OF GENESIS 2

Let's take a moment to recall the natural flow of rivers because we will use the four rivers of Genesis 2 in an attempt to locate the Garden of Eden. We'll consider the major rivers in America. Typical water flow for rivers is that tributary waterways come together and feed into a single river. Take the Mighty Mississippi River as an example. If you follow it from its beginning in Minnesota to the location where it pours into the Gulf of Mexico, multiple tributary rivers such as the Ohio River, the Missouri River, and the Arkansas River feed into it. This is the exact opposite of the flow of the rivers of the second chapter of Genesis. Instead of multiple tributary rivers flowing into and feeding one main river, the Bible states that the one main river flowed out of Eden and fed four tributary rivers. This simple fact of the direction of the river's water flow is vital in that the rivers of the second chapter of Genesis flowed in an opposite direction of what we know the majority of rivers today. This fact will be revisited a little later in our search for the Garden.

We will begin our examination of the four rivers being fed from Eden by looking first at the Euphrates and the Hiddekel because it is generally agreed that these two rivers are the present-day Euphrates and Tigris Rivers. And although they may not flow exactly as they flowed 10,000 years ago, they would still be in the general geographical region that they were then. The Euphrates is referred to in the original biblical text as "Prat", the Hebrew rendition of the Babylonian and Assyrian words for the river located next to the city of Babylon. Again, most modern translations of the Bible say "Euphrates" without further explanation. The present-day Euphrates River flows from the mountains of Turkey, down through Syria and Iraq, then empties into the Persian Gulf. It merges with the Tigris River in southern

Iraq, just before emptying into the gulf. The present-day Tigris River also heads, or starts, in Turkey, then just as the Euphrates, flows south through the northeast tip of Syria, then into Iraq, where it merges with the Euphrates, just north of the Persian Gulf.

PRESENT DAY EUPHRATES AND TIGRIS RIVERS

Most experts agree that the present-day Tigris River is the Hiddekel River of Genesis 2. This matching of the modern-day Tigris River with the biblical Hiddekel River is largely based on Daniel providing his location when he received a vision from God.[xxi] Daniel stated that he was by the side of the 'great River Hiddekel'. Since we know that Daniel was taken to Babylon (present-day Iraq) when Nebuchadnezzar overtook Israel, if Daniel was standing by the Hiddekel

River, this river had to flow through the Babylonian region. So the first two rivers, which have retained their names to this day, are in present-day Mesopotamia. Their flow may have extended further, flowed in different directions, etc., 10,000 years ago. But knowing their current location in the world is a start because these two rivers somewhat narrow the location of the Garden of Eden to the Mesopotamia region of the world.

But there are no known traces of the other two rivers anywhere near the area of these two, and that complicates locating Eden using only these two rivers.

We should also keep in mind that since Adam and Eve were evicted from the garden, the earth experienced the great flood of Noah's time, and it is generally believed that water levels rose and remained higher after the flood than they were before the flood. So other rivers may have existed at the time but are now under one of the Seas located in the area. But locating Eden becomes even more complicated when we consider these remaining two rivers mentioned in the second chapter of Genesis.

The other two rivers are less well known than the Euphrates and the Hiddekel, and herein is the problem of solely using the four rivers to determine where the Garden of Eden was located. The names of these two rivers, Gihon and Pison, are not in existence today. But the bible names the countries associated with these rivers and the countries that are confidently known to us today. The Bible says that the Gihon

River surrounded the land of Ethiopia or Cush, while the Pison River flowed around the land of Havilah. As for the land of Ethiopia, we know that it was, and still is, in Africa and the Bible seems to connect it with Mesopotamia (Genesis 10:8).

We should first define the word 'Ethiopia' because it will be relevant throughout this book. The word Ethiopia is a Greek word meaning 'of burnt face' or black face[xxii]. Throughout the Bible, the word Ethiopia is used when referring to the descendants of Ham through Cush, or the Cushites. So, whereas the country Ethiopia would be the African nation, the word Ethiopians would refer to all black people, as all black people would be native to or descendants of the Cushites, who occupied the country. This word 'Ethiopians' is synonymous with the indigenous Cushites or black Africans, from whom African Americans descended. So when the bible and biblical texts mention the 'Ethiopians', or people of Ethiopia, it refers specifically to 'black' descendants of Cush. So the Gihon River surrounded the country of Ethiopia, the land of the indigenous black people in Africa.

The Pison River is also named, and it is said of this river that it "compasseth the whole land of Havilah". Many bible scholars believe that the land of Havilah was located somewhere northwest of Ethiopia in Africa. We know that in biblical times, just as today, many regions, nations, countries, etc., were named for the indigenous people who initially inherited the land. Hence, the *'land of Havilah'* would be so named because it was the homeland of the indigenous people to the land where Havilah and his descendants resided. We find in 1 Chronicles 1:9 that Havilah was the son of Cush, the grandson of Ham, and the great-grandson of Noah. This makes Havilah an indigenous African.

1 Chronicles 1:9

> "⁹And the sons of Cush; Seba, and **Havilah**, and Sabtah, and Raamah, and Sabtecha. And the sons of Raamah; Sheba, and Dedan."

Other scripture, such as Genesis 25:18 and 1 Samuel 15:7, provides undeniable support that Havilah was in Africa. This would make Havilah '***Biblically Black***' because Cush is synonymous with Ethiopia and the indigenous Africans. This would place the river Pison somewhere in the eastern region of Africa between Ethiopia and Egypt. We are also informed that Havilah has Gold, bdellium, and the onyx stone.

The fact that the Bible specifies the riches of Havilah are important because we know that Africa today is rich in precious metals, minerals, and other valuable natural resources. So it is plausible that the Pison River is, as many believe, the modern-day Nile River. When I began exploring the rivers, I noted that the flow of these rivers was the opposite of most modern-day rivers for which we have knowledge. Instead of tributary rivers feeding into the main river, the Bible lets us know of these rivers that they flowed just the opposite: the main river flowed into, or fed, four tributaries. An interesting note here is that the modern-day Nile River flows from South to North instead of North to South.

PRESENT DAY NILE RIVER

Other bible scholars theorize that the Pison River is the modern-day Ganges River that flows across North-Eastern India. This theory places the land of Havilah in Northern India. But this further complicates using the four rivers to locate the Garden because there is no point of confluence of the Ganges River with the previous two rivers, the Euphrates and the Tigris Rivers. Neither is their confluence of this Ganges River with any river or landmass located in present-day Africa.

PRESENT DAY GANGES RIVER

Of the four rivers we will look at, the bible provides the most accurate location information about the Gihon River. Even though the river itself is no longer in existence, the bible says of the Gihon River that it "compasseth the whole land of Ethiopia", or it surrounded the country of Ethiopia. One thing that is generally agreed upon by bible and geological scholars is that the location of modern-day Ethiopia is generally the same today as it was in biblical times. Since the Gihon River flows around Ethiopia, we can, with assurance, say that the Gihon River was located in Africa and quite possibly could be what is known today as the Nile and the Blue Nile Rivers.

ETHIOPIA WITH NILE AND BLUE NILE RIVERS

So you can see that it is futile at best to use the rivers of Genesis 2 as the sole basis for locating Eden. Of the four rivers named, only two of the rivers are in existence today (Hiddekel and Euphrates). There is uncertainty as to whether they have maintained their direction, flow, and length; whereas of the two countries associated with the other two rivers, Havilah and Ethiopia, one of the countries, Ethiopia, is in existence today, and we can with assurance locate the other (Havilah). Both countries are located on the

African continent. Since the two rivers that we can locate today are in Mesopotamia, the two countries associated with the other two rivers are located in Africa. We can only hypothesize about the biblical direction, flow, and location while making assumptions based on the present-day topology in the region.

Therefore, we can conclude that solely using the rivers of Genesis 2 to locate Eden provides us with a location that ranges from modern-day Turkey in the north, all the way south into Africa and, more specifically, Ethiopia. This narrows the search for Eden in respect to the world but still leaves us with a large geographical area that could have been home to Eden. So after examining the rivers, we still can't pinpoint Eden. We can only place Eden somewhere between Turkey in the north and Ethiopia (Africa) in the south.

I will take a moment here and introduce the Pangean Theory. Many historians believe this theory could provide more specificity to the location of the Garden. The Pangean Theory is a theory that holds that the earth was once a single 'super-continent' and over the period of millions, maybe even billions, of years, this super-continent broke apart and expanded into the seven continents that we know today. Take a good look at the following diagrams.

BIBLICALLY BLACK & BLESSED

PANGEAN EARTH WITH UNITED STATES HIGHLIGHTED

EXPANDED EARTH WITH UNITED STATES

In the previous diagrams, I have outlined the United States on both the Pangean Earth and the Expanded Earth (earth as we know it today). When looking at the seven continents, you can see how the seven continents could have fit together as a single super-continent. A Pangean Earth, as shown in the following picture, would have brought the two known rivers of Genesis 2 into close proximity of the two known countries associated with the other two rivers.

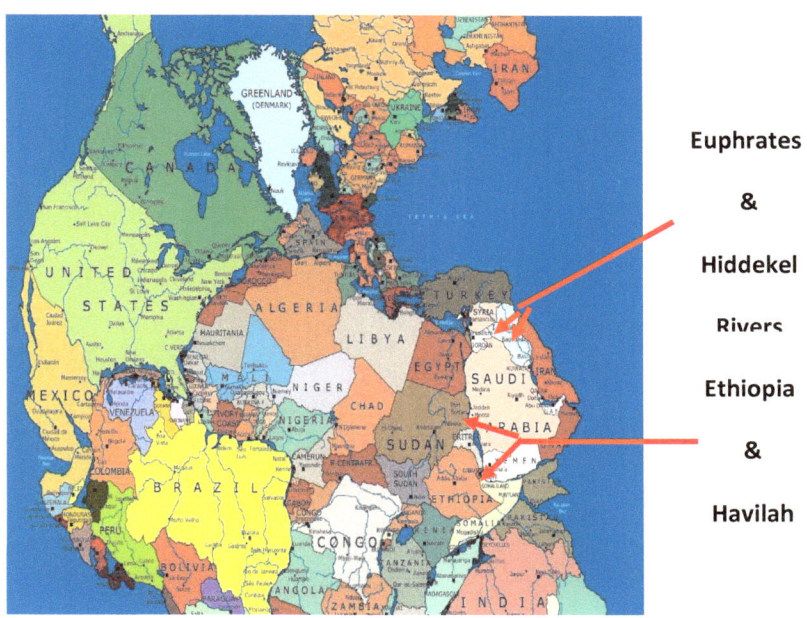

PANGEAN EARTH WITH THE RIVERS OF GENESIS 2 IDENTIFIED

The Pangean Earth theory is plausible because it is highly likely, even probable, that the earth was once a single super-continent. Since it would take hundreds of millions of years for this super-continent to break apart and expand, this expansion would have occurred during the time between the time in which God created the heaven and the earth (Genesis 1:1), and the time in which He re-organized the heaven and earth after the fall of Satan (Genesis 1:2 – 19). We can confidently assert, with biblical support, that Adam dates back only about 10,000 years, and this would not be enough time for the Pangean continent to expand into the seven continents that we know today. Remember, according to Isaiah 14, Satan's fall shook the earth, causing it to be void and without form. This shaking of the earth would have broken apart the super-continent and created the seven continents as we know them today. But since God planted the Garden of Eden and placed man in it after that, the Pangean Theory has no impact on our search for Eden.

But there is science that can be applied to provide an even narrower area where the Garden of Eden would have been located. Applying this science to our knowledge of the four rivers of Genesis 2, we can locate the continent and identify the region on that continent where God placed Eden.

The Black Adam and Eve of The Bible

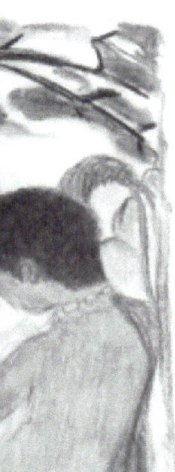

"And Adam said, this is now bone of my bones, and flesh of my flesh: she shall be called Woman, because she was taken out of Man." [xxiii]

With this statement, Adam gave a name to the female gender of the human species that God formed by taking one of his ribs. I mention this only because the way God formed Eve would mean that she had Adam's DNA. Therefore, locating

Eden could be possible if, by some method, we could perform DNA screening on all ethnic groups and identify commonalities that connect them all. I am not a scientist, nor am I a geneticist or DNA expert, so I will refer to the work of noted Geneticist Rebecca Cann that was published by Newsweek in January of 1998.[xxiv]

Dr. Cann applied DNA testing to women of every core ethnic origin in existence today and concluded that "Eve …was more likely a dark-haired, black-skinned woman, roaming a hot savanna in search of food." The research stated that Dr. Cann's team of trained molecular biologists "looked at an international assortment of genes and picked up a trail of DNA that led them to a single woman from whom we all descended. Most evidence so far indicates that Eve lived in sub-Saharan Africa."

January 1988 Cover of Newsweek

The rivers of Genesis 2 narrow the possible locations of The Garden of Eden from the entire world to an area where God may have planted the Garden of Eden, Dr. Cann's DNA research further narrows this area to 'sub-Saharan Africa'. These scientists went on to say:

"Her (Eve) genes seem to be in all humans living today: 5 billion blood relatives. She was, by one rough estimate, your 10,000th-great-grandmother."

In support of this, at the writing of this book, the oldest known evidence for anatomically modern humans are fossils found at Jebel Irhoud, Morocco[xxv]. Keep in mind that Morocco is a country in Northern Africa. Although I will disagree with the age that these scientists have calculated for these fossils, there can be no disagreement that they are the oldest fossils of modern humans. As long as the method for determining age is consistent when applied to all fossils, the determined difference in age will be consistent when referenced to other fossils on which the same method is applied. Therefore, any disagreement will not be a disagreement in the difference in age of the fossils, but the disagreement is in respect to the reference point in which the determination of the age was started. In other words, if I say you are the oldest person in the room, I am saying that you were born before everyone else in the room. We can disagree on the year in which you were born, but regardless of what year you were born, it will still be prior to the birth year of everyone else in the room. So I can disagree with these scientists on the year in which this fossil was a living human, but since the same method used on this fossil was applied to other fossils, we can agree that these are indeed the oldest.

Now there are other fossils that have been unearthed in Ethiopia and other sub-Saharan regions of Africa. You may even remember the excitement generated when the fossils named 'Lucy' were found. These fossils date back hundreds of thousands of years, and as such, they would be fossils of 'Creature' and not 'Man'. Remember, earlier we stated that 'Creature' may have had many man-like features and characteristics, but he was not a '*Living Soul*' and as such was not made in God's image, thus rendering him incapable and unqualified to be classified as 'Man'.

With this we see that the four rivers of Genesis chapter 2 provide a very wide area in which the Garden of Eden could have been placed. But the scientific DNA research performed by Dr. Rebecca Cann and a team of Biological Geneticists narrowed this area to Africa while concluding that Eve was a dark-skinned African woman that was indigenous to sub-Saharan Africa. Adding to this, the oldest fossilized remains of modern man has been unearthed in the North African country of Morocco. With this evidence, we can confidently state that the Garden of Eden was located on the continent of Africa and Eve was an indigenous black African woman. Since Eve was taken from Adam, we can, therefore with confidence say that Adam too, was a black man indigenous to the continent of Africa.[xxvi]

We can therefore establish with reasonable certainty that the Garden of Eden was located on the African continent. But where? Of the seven continents, Africa is by far the largest. And current Mercator world maps were drawn mainly to assist in the navigation of the seas and are wildly misleading. These maps are also biased to minimize the landmass that is the continent of Africa.

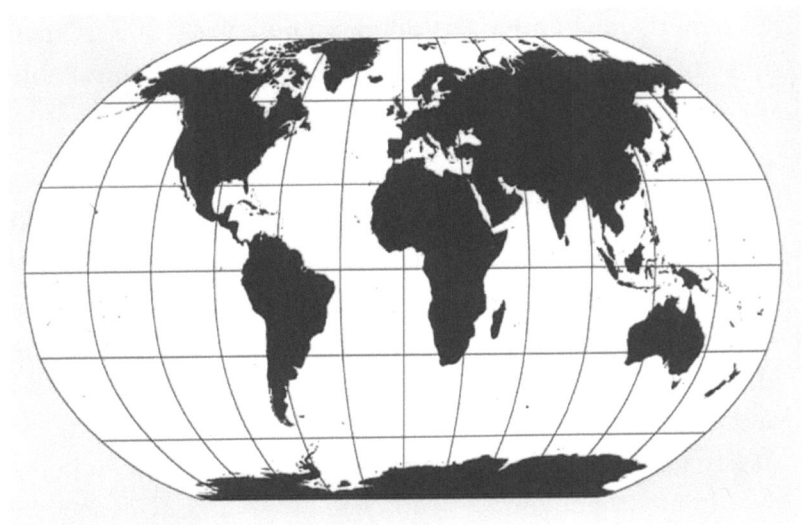

MERCATOR MAP SHOWING AFRICA AND THE WORLD

MAP SHOWING ACTUAL SIZE OF AFRICA

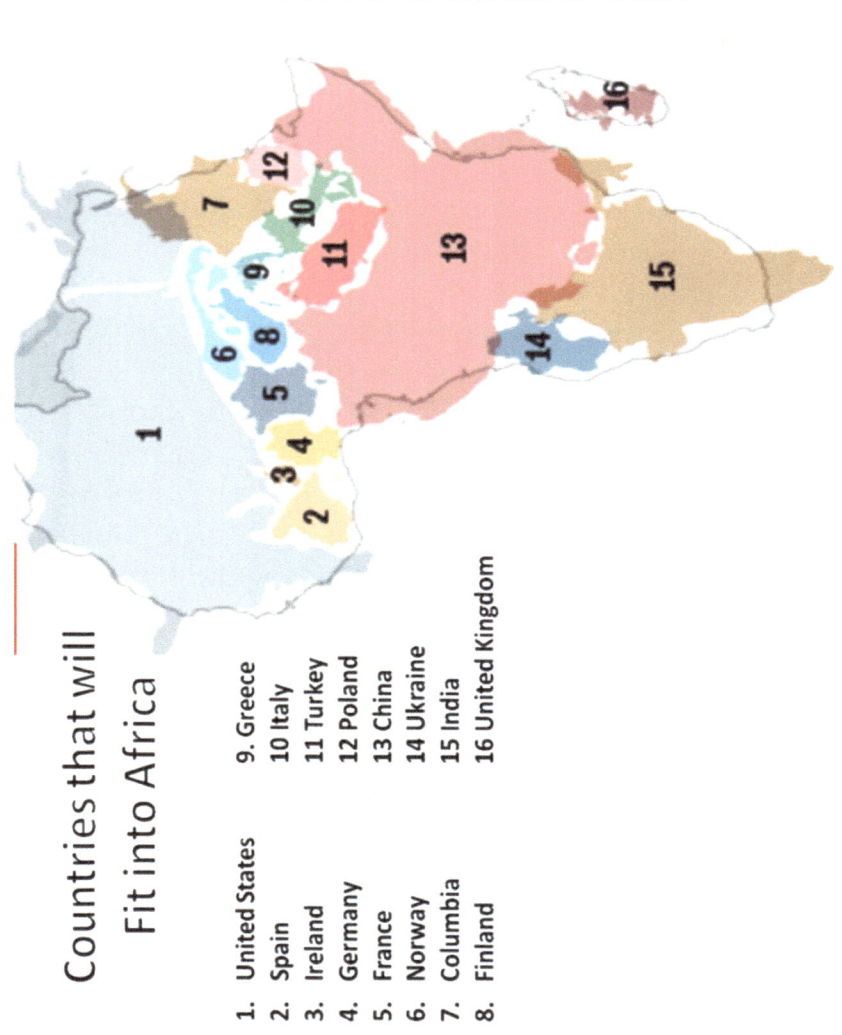

CNN Graphic

With such an enormous landmass, locating the Garden of Eden on Africa's continent establishes that Adam and Eve were dark-skinned people. Still, the indigenous people of Africa have skin colors that range from light brown (Northern Africa) to dark brown or bronze (Central Africa) to Black (Southern Africa).

Although the exact location of Eden on the African continent cannot be identified, the location of the land and rivers provides us with enough clues to make an educated estimation. Ethiopia is the only country named in Genesis 2 that exists today by its same name and location. It is this author's belief that the Garden of Eden was located in present-day Ethiopia. Acknowledging that the geographical topology has changed, the Blue Nile flows out of Ethiopia, making it the unnamed river that flowed out of the Garden. The four heads that it supplied were the Nile River, the Euphrates, and Tigris Rivers, which would have flowed farther south and westward before the topology changed. The Ganges River, which would have extended farther east prior to topology change. I believe that this is the primary reason Ethiopia is one of only two African countries that violently resisted colonization by the Gentile nations. God would not allow this precious country to fall under Gentile rule. Although Ethiopia has persevered through many difficult, complex, and trying periods, and they continue to struggle, they were selected by God when He created man. God will never forsake them. Many of the issues and obstacles that confront Ethiopia are manmade. They are the result of discrimination by the Gentile nations and an attempt to isolate Ethiopia and thereby force them into submission simply because they successfully resisted colonization.

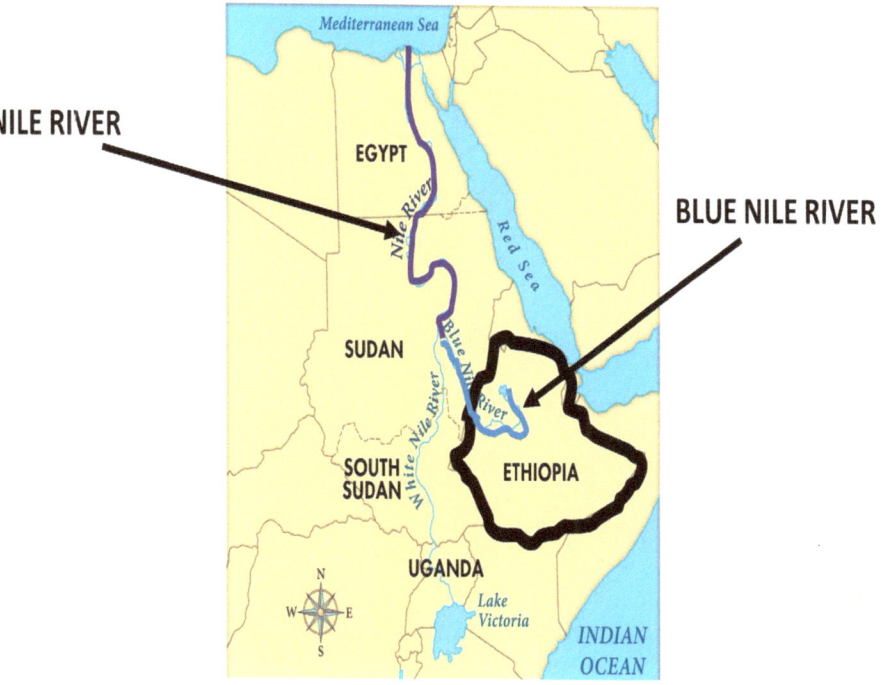

Black People – The Descendants of Ham Through Cush

"And the sons of Noah, that went forth of the ark, were Shem, and Ham, and Japheth: and Ham is the father of Canaan. These are the three sons of Noah: and of them was the whole earth overspread."[xxvii]

After Adam and Eve were evicted from the Garden, they begin to reproduce, and sin was immediately present. Their first child Cain committed the first murder and attempted to cover it up. As the population of the earth increased, sin proportionately increased. Man was sinning at such a pace that God said it grieved Him that he made man and placed him upon the earth. God purposed to destroy man from the earth and start all over. And since Noah was the only just and righteous man on the face of the earth, it was with Noah that God would re-populate the earth after he destroyed all mankind. And in the midst of the great sin of man, God caused a great flood to overtake the earth, and only Noah, his family, and the animals were saved in the ark. But after the flood, the earth again needed to be re-populated, and the responsibility for this fell to Noah's sons.

The Bible tells us that Noah's sons went forth from the ark and by them "was the whole earth overspread". So everyone has a direct genetic link back to Noah through one of his sons and from Noah back to Adam. All of the races, ethnicities and genetic lineages can therefore be traced back to one of Noah's three sons. This brings us to two of the greatest chapters in the Bible…Genesis Chapter 10 and 11. The tenth and eleventh chapters of Genesis are often referred to as the table of nations. It is in these chapters that we identify the lineages of all current races and ethnicities.

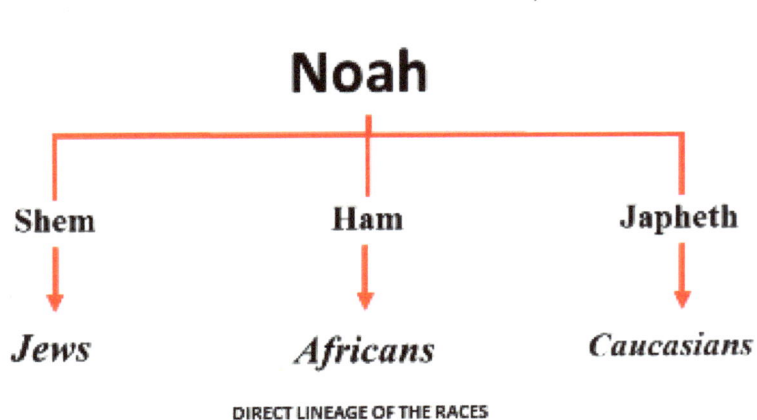

DIRECT LINEAGE OF THE RACES

We must note here that Noah was only ten generations removed from Adam. Since Adam and Eve were evicted from the Garden of Eden in Africa, by the time of Noah, man had not traveled far from their place of origin. This would mean that Noah and his three sons would have the same or similar skin color as Adam and Eve. It is also important to note that Noah gave birth to three sons who became three nations, NOT THREE RACES! Noah's sons were not of three different skin colors; they were all dark-skinned. The races developed as the sons traveled from the equator, from their African place of origin, and settled in other regions of the world. Respected Anthropologist Nina Jablonski theorized that "variations in human skin are adaptive traits that correlate closely to geography and the sun's ultraviolet radiation, **not race.** Over the course of human development, human ancestors became bigger and more active as they moved into hot, open environments in search of food and water. In these places, one big challenge was keeping cool. The adaptation they made was to increase the number of sweat glands on their skin while at the same time reducing the amount of their body hair," explains Jablonski. "With less hair, perspiration could evaporate more easily and cool the body more efficiently. But this less-hairy skin was a problem because it was exposed to very strong sun, especially in lands near the equator. Strong sun exposure damages the body. The solution was to evolve skin that was permanently dark so as to protect against the sun's more damaging rays"[xxviii]. Dr. Jablonski's research is performed using a Caucasian person as the reference. But this is science, and the process would also hold true in the reverse if a dark-skinned person, a black person, is used as the reference. If human skin evolved or adapted to the climate, then dark skin with less hair would become lighter in color and hairier as the people migrated north away from the equator. Dark skin exists because God created man and placed him in a hot climate near the equator. The Almighty and All-Knowing God knew that humans living in hot climates would need protection from the sun, so He equipped them with dark skin that naturally provides this protection. Jablonski went on to say, "As some groups moved into regions farther from the equator where UVR levels are lower, natural selection favored lighter skin, which allowed enough vitamin D-forming UVR to penetrate their skin."

This would account for lighter hairier skin in regions farther from the equator because protection is needed from the colder temperature. This provides the explanation for the indigenous darker skin people being native to Sub Saharan Africa, whereas the indigenous lighter-skinned people being native to regions in the northern hemisphere and the indigenous tan skinned people being native to the Northern Africa and Mesopotamia regions of the world.

HENRY L. RAZOR

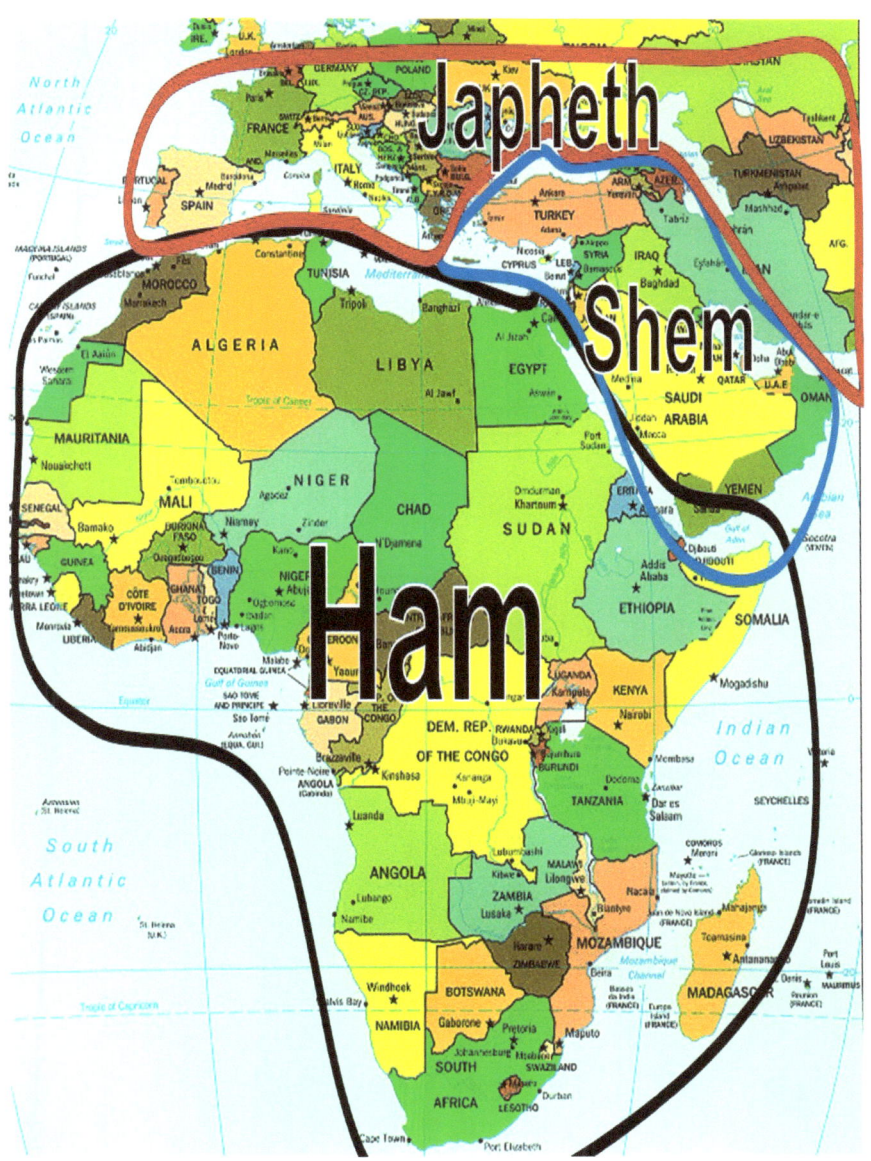

The Settlement of Noah's Sons After The Flood

Let's take a look at the output of the Table of Nations.

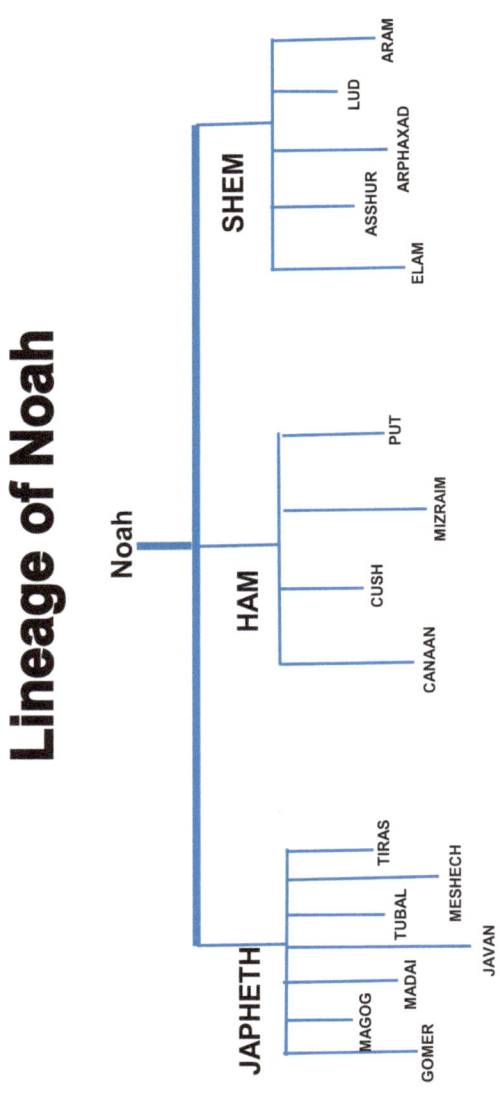

SHEM

(*Sons & Their Lineage*)

- **Elam** *(sons were Shushan, Machul and Harmon)* - *(Elamites, Persians);*
- **Asshur** *(sons were Mirus and Mokil)* - *(Assyrians/Northern Iraqis);*
- **Arphaxad** *(sons were Shelach, Anar and Ashcol)* - *(Chaldeans/Southern Iraqis, Hebrews/Israelites/Jews, Arabians/Bedouins, Moabites/Jordanians/Palestinians*
- **Lud** *(sons were Pethor and Bizayon)* - *(Ludim, Lubim, Ludians, Ludu, Lydians, Chubs, other groups in Asia and North Africa);*
- **Aram** *(sons were Uz, Chul, Gather and Mash)* - *(Aramaeans/<u>Syrians, Lebanese</u>, and some groups in Asia, and North Africa.*

BIBLICALLY BLACK & BLESSED

HAM

(*Sons & Their Lineage*)

- **Canaan** *(sons were Zidon1, Heth, Amori, Gergashi, Hivi, Arkee, Seni, Arodi, Zimodi and Chamothi) - also Canaanites, Cana, Chna, Chanani, Chanana, Canaana, Kana, Kenaanah, Kena'ani, Kena'an, Kn'nw, Kyn'nw, Kinnahu, Kinahhi, Kinahni, Kinahna, Kinahne (Mongols, Chinese, Taiwanese, Thais, Vietnamese, Japanese, Asians, Eskimos, American Indians, Malayasians, Indonesians, Filipinos, Hawaiians, Polynesians, Tahitians, Guamanians, Samoans, Fijians, Tongans, Pacific Islanders*
- **Cush** *(sons were Seba, Havilah, Sabta, Raama and Satecha) - also Chus, Kush, Kosh* (**Nubians, Ethiopians, Ghanaians, Africans**, *Bushmen, Pygmies, Australian Aborignies, New Guineans*
- **Mizraim** *(sons were Lud, Anom, Pathros, Chasloth and Chaphtor) - also Misraim, Mitzraim, Mizraite, Mitsrayim* **Egyptians**, *Khemets, Copts*
- **Phut** *(sons were Gebul, Hadan, Benah and Adan) - also Punt, Puta, Put, Puni, Phoud, Pul, Fula, Putaya, Putiya, Libia, Libya* (**Libyans**, *Cyrenacians, Tunisians, Berbers, Somalians, Sudanese, North Africans).*

The people in other parts of Africa, Arabia, Asia, the aboriginal Australians, Pacific Islanders, American Indians and Eskimos also descended from Canaan, Cush, Mizraim and Phut.

JAPHETH

(Sons & Their Lineage)

- **Gomer** *(sons were Ashkenaz, Riphath and Togarmah) - also Gamir, Gommer, Gomeri, Gomeria, Gomery, Goth, Guth, Gutar, Götar, Gadelas, Galic, Gallic, Galicia, Galica, Galatia, Gael, Getae, Galatae, Galatoi, Gaul, Galls, Goar, Celt, Celtae, Celticae, Kelt, Keltoi, Gimmer, Gimmerai, Gimirra, Gimirrai, Gimirraya, Kimmer, Kimmeroi, Kimirraa, Kumri, Umbri, Cimmer, Cimmeria, Cimbri, Cimbris, Crimea, Chomari, Cymric, Cymry, Cymru, Cymbry, Cumber (Caledonians, Picts, Milesians, Umbrians, Helvetians, Celts1, Galatians, Ostrogoths, Visigoths, Goths, Vandals, Scandinavians, Jutes, Teutons, Franks, Burgundians, Alemanni, Armenians, Germans, Belgians, Dutch, Luxembourgers, Liechensteiners, Austrians, Swiss, Angles, Saxons, Britons, English, Cornish, Irish, Welsh, French*
- **Tiras** *(sons were Benib, Gera, Lupirion and Gilak) - also Tiracian, Thracian, Thirasian, Thuras, Troas, Tros, Troia, Troi, Troy, Trajan, Trojan, Taunrus, Tyrsen, Tyrrhena, Rasenna, Tursha, Tusci, Tuscany, Etruscan, Eturscan, Erul, Herul, Heruli, Erilar, Vanir, Danir, Daner, Aesar, Aesir, Asir, Svear, Svea, Svie, Svioner, Svenonian, Urmane, Norge (Pelasgians, Scandinavians7, Varangians, Vikings, Swedes, Norwegians, Danes, Icelandics*

JAPHETH

(Sons & Their Lineage cont.)

- **Magog** *(sons were Elichanaf, Lubal, Baath, Jobhath and Fathochta) - also Gog, Gogh, Jagog, Agag, Magug, Magogae, Mugogh, Mat Gugi, Gugu, Gyges, Bedwig, Moghef, Magogian, Massagetae, Dacae, Sacae, Scyth, Scythi, Scythii, Scythia, Scythae, Sythia, Scythes, Skuthai, Skythai, Cathaia, Scythia, Skythia, Scynthia, Scynthius, Sclaveni, Samartian, Scoloti, Skodiai, Scotti, Skoloti, Skoth-ai, Skoth, Skuthes, Skuth-a, Askuza, Askuasa, Alani, Alans, Alanic, Ulan, Uhlan (Scythians, Scots, Irish); also Rasapu, Rashu, Rukhs, Rukhs-As, Rhos, Ros, Rosh, Rox, Roxolani, Rhoxolani, Ruskolan, Rosichi, Rhossi, Rusichi, Rus, Ruska, Rossiya, Rusian (Russians, Belarusians, Ukrainians); also Mas-ar, Mas-gar, Masgar, Mazar, Madj, Madjar, Makr-on, Makar, Makaroi, Merkar, Magor, Magar, Magyar (Hungarians - also Hungar, Hunugur, Hurri, Gurri, Onogur, Ugor, Ungar, Uhor, Venger); Finns, Lapps, Estonians, Siberians, Yugoslavians, Croatians, Bosnians, Montenegrins, Serbians, Slovenians, Slovakians, Bulgarians, Poles, Czechs*
- **Madai** *(sons were Achon, Zeelo, Chazoni and Lotalso) - also Mada, Amada, Madae, Madea, Manda, Maday, Media, Madaean, Mata, Matiene, Mitani, Mitanni, Megala (Medes, Aryans, Persians, Parsa, Parsees, Achaemenians, Manneans, Caspians, Kassites, Iranians, Kurds, Turks, East Indians, Pathans, Hazaras), including the peoples of Afghanistan, Pakistan, Azerbaijan, Khazachstan, Turkmenistan, Uzbekistan, Tajikistan and Kyrgyzstan*

JAPHETH

(Sons & Their Lineage cont.)

- **Javan** *(sons were Elisha, Tarshish, Kittim and Dodanim)* - *also Jevanim, Iewanim, Iawan, Iawon, Iamanu, Iones, Ionians, Ellas, Ellines, El-li-ness, Hellas, Hellenes, Yavan, Yavanas, Yawan, Yuban, Yauna, Uinivu, Xuthus (Grecians, Greeks, Elysians, Spartans, Dorians, Britons, Aeolians, Achaeans, Myceneans, Macedonians, Carthaginians, Cyprians, Cretans, Basques, Latins, Venetians, Sicanians, Italics, Romans, Valentians, Sicilians, Italians, Spaniards, Portugese*
- **Tubal** *(sons were Ariphi, Kesed and Taari) - also Tabal, Tabali, Tubalu, Tbilisi, Tibarenoi, Tibareni, Tibar, Tibor, Sabir, Sapir, Sabarda, Subar, Subartu, Thobal, Thobel, Tobol, Tobolsk ,Georgians, Albanians*
- **Meshech** *(sons were Dedon, Zaron and Shebashnialso) - Me'shech, Mes'ek, Meshekh, Meshwesh, Meskhi, Mushch, Muschki, Mushki, Mishi, Muski, Mushku, Musku, Muskeva, Muska, Muskaa, Muskai, Maskali, Machar, Maskouci, Mazakha, Mazaca, Massagatae, Mtskhetos, Modar-es, Moskhi, Moshkhi, Mosah, Mosher, Moshch, Moschis, Mosoch, Moschi, Moschian, Moshakian, Mo'skhoi, Moschoi, Mosochenu, Mosochean, Mossynes, Mosynoeci, Moskva, Moscovy, Moscow (Muscovites, Latvians, Lithuanians, Romanians*

As you analyze the output of these tables, the major obvious genealogical output shows that:

1. Shem is the father of the indigenous Jews and Arabs
2. Ham is the father of the indigenous Africans and Black people through Cush
3. Japheth is the father of the indigenous Caucasians

Also standing out is the number of ethnic groups that are descendants of Japheth. Many of the groups are not populous, but they are many. This is a very good place to analyze who Japheth really is relative to the bible. The descendants of Japheth are the 'Gentiles'. That's right, when the bible speaks of the Gentiles; it is referring specifically to the Caucasians who are the descendants of Japheth.

Genesis 10:1-5

> ¹Now these are the generations of the sons of Noah, Shem, Ham, and Japheth: and unto them were sons born after the flood.
>
> ² The sons of Japheth; Gomer, and Magog, and Madai, and Javan, and Tubal, and Meshech, and Tiras.
>
> ³ And the sons of Gomer; Ashkenaz, and Riphath, and Togarmah.
>
> ⁴ And the sons of Javan; Elishah, and Tarshish, Kittim, and Dodanim.

> ⁵ By these were the isles of the Gentiles divided in their lands; every one after his tongue, after their families, in their nations.

While analyzing the number of ethnic groups that proceeded from Japheth, consider that these represent the gentile nations.

Many teach that a gentile is anyone that is NOT of Jewish descent. But according to the bible, the descendants of Ham are not gentiles. That's right; black people are not gentiles. This will be re-visited when we look at God's relationship with black people, but for now, we will simply say that when the bible speaks about the activities, atrocities, evils, and ungodliness of the Gentiles, it is referring specifically to the offspring of Japheth.

1 Peter 4:3-5(KJV)

> ³ For the time past of our life may suffice us to have wrought the will of the Gentiles, when we walked in lasciviousness, lusts, excess of wine, revellings, banquetings, and abominable idolatries:
>
> ⁴ Wherein they think it strange that ye run not with them to the same excess of riot, speaking evil of you:
>
> ⁵ Who shall give account to him that is ready to judge the quick and the dead.

BIBLICALLY BLACK & BLESSED

1 Corinthians 10:20 (KJV)

> [20] But I say, that the things which the Gentiles sacrifice, they sacrifice to devils, and not to God: and I would not that ye should have fellowship with devils.

For this book, the focus is on the descendants of Ham, or the indigenous black people. Ham's descendants remained in the general area of The Garden of Eden (Africa) and Mesopotamia, whereas his brothers move out from the region and adapted to the environment where they settled. Ham's descendants remained dark skinned whereas the descendants of his bothers became lighter and hairier as they ventured farther away from the equator. Black people have a rich spiritual history that can only be attributed to our dedication to God and the longevity and strength of our relationship with God. Let's examine Ham's descendants and the topology of their land.

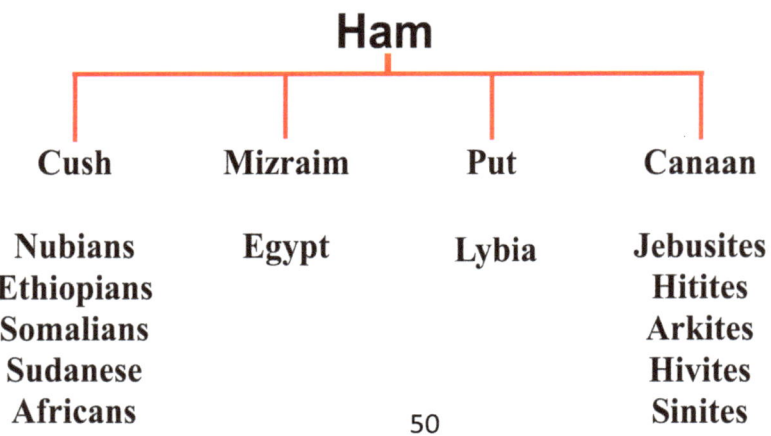

The first thing that must be acknowledged and accepted when identifying indigenous black people of the bible and placing them in their indigenous homelands is the proper geography and topology of the continent of Africa. Today we hear a lot about the 'Middle East'. But there is no continent, country, or region that bears that name. The Middle East is a transcontinental region that <u>includes</u> northern Africa. Egypt and Libya are mentioned so often in the context of the Middle East that all too often, we overlook the fact that they are in Africa. So when identifying Ham's indigenous descendants, we must always keep in mind that Egypt and Libya are as much 'Africa' as Ethiopia, Somalia, and Sudan. If we remain mindful of this, it will be much easier to understand the relationship with God that Ham's descendants have enjoyed for thousands of years.

BIBLICALLY BLACK & BLESSED

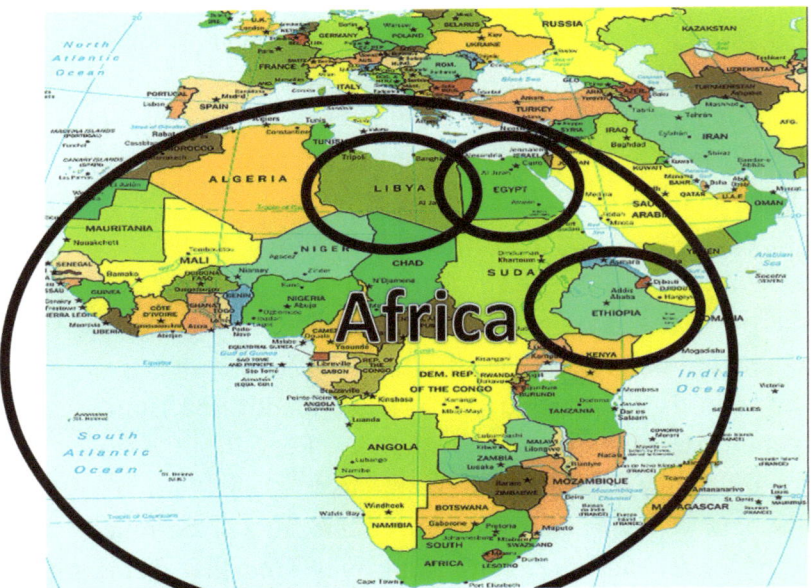

MAP OF AFRICA AND MIDDLE EAST REGION WITH LIBYA, EGYPT, AND ETHIOPIA HIGHLIGHTED

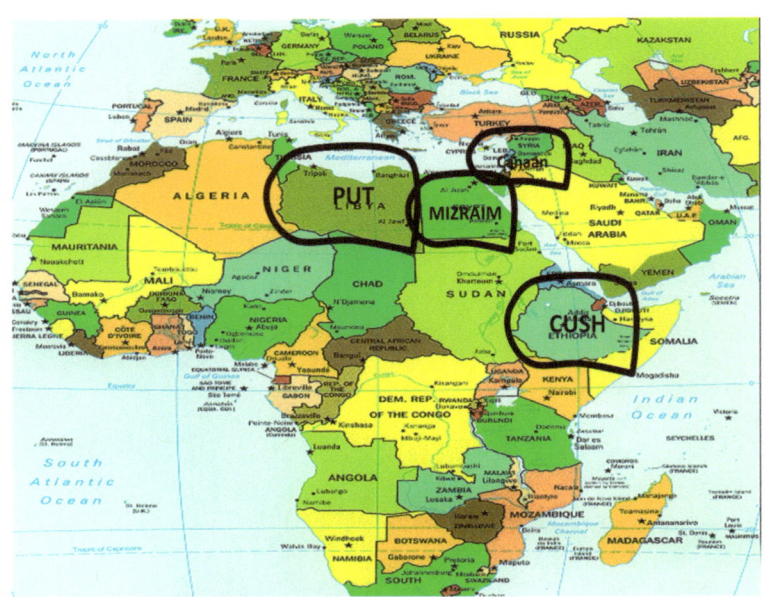

MAP OF AFRICA AND MIDDLE EAST REGION WITH SONS OF HAM HIGHLIGHTED

MAP OF THE MIDDLE EAST WITH AFRICAN NATIONS HIGHLIGHTED

Genesis chapter ten and verse six reads" "And the sons of Ham; Cush, and Mizraim, and Put, and Canaan." Note from the previous chart that the sons of Ham directly correlate to African nations. As stated earlier, the indigenous black people, also known as the descendants of Ham, have skin color that ranges from light brown or tan to black. They can all be accounted for within the direct lineage of one of Ham's sons. But the Cushites, or Ethiopians, were darker than the descendants of Mizraim, Put, or even Canaan's descendants. The Bible provides evidence that the Cushites were not of the same skin color as the descendants of Shem, Japheth, or even Mizraim, Put, and Canaan after they hadnmigrated further from the equator into northern Africa, nor did they have the same skin color as Canaan after he migrated into the Mesopotamian region.

Jeremiah 13:23 KJV

> ²³Can the Ethiopian change his skin, or the leopard his spots? then may ye also do good, that are accustomed to do evil.

Keep in mind, as earlier stated, that all of Noah's sons are nations, NOT RACES. Noah did not have sons that were diverse in skin color, but Ham's descendants remained in the region near the equator, where God first created man, so they retained the natural skin color of the first man. Ham's brothers, however, ventured out and re-located in other African regions, and over time, their skin color adapted to a color that is suitable for survival in those regions.

When we follow the ethnic descendants of Ham's son, we also find that Ham's seed was prominent in the lineage of Jesus.

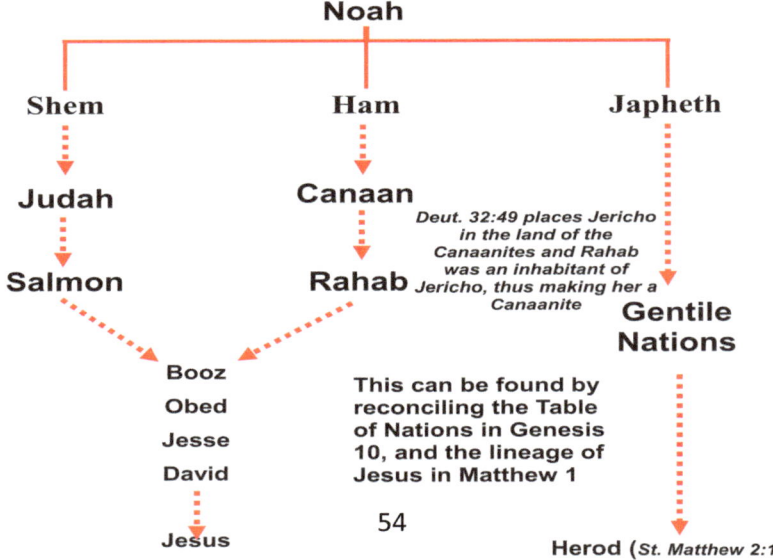

So you may be wondering '*How Could This Be? Wasn't Ham cursed?*' I will take a moment here to explain the sin committed by Ham and the curse imposed by Noah because I have encountered much misunderstanding relative to this incident.

Genesis 9:20-27 KJV

> [20] And Noah began to be an husbandman, and he planted a vineyard:
>
> [21] And he drank of the wine, and was drunken; and he was uncovered within his tent.
>
> [22] And Ham, the father of Canaan, saw the nakedness of his father, and told his two brethren without.
>
> [23] And Shem and Japheth took a garment, and laid it upon both their shoulders, and went backward, and covered the nakedness of their father; and their faces were backward, and they saw not their father's nakedness.
>
> [24] And Noah awoke from his wine, and knew what his younger son had done unto him.
>
> [25] And he said, Cursed be Canaan; a servant of servants shall he be unto his brethren.
>
> [26] And he said, Blessed be the Lord God of Shem; and Canaan shall be his servant.

> ²⁷ God shall enlarge Japheth, and he shall dwell in the tents of Shem; and Canaan shall be his servant.

The sin committed by Ham was that he "saw the nakedness of his father", or he 'uncovered his father's nakedness'. Many have speculated as to what 'saw the nakedness of his father' really meant. But the bible gives us a pretty clear definition of this sin, and once we accept that, it becomes apparent why Noah cursed Canaan. To understand the sin and the curse, we must first know what is meant by 'the nakedness of his father'. Note here that the wording is 'the nakedness of his father', and not 'Noah's nakedness', or not even 'the nakedness of Noah.

Leviticus 20:11 KJV

> ¹¹ And the man that lieth with his father's wife hath uncovered his father's nakedness:

It is clear here that a man's wife is considered by God to be that man's nakedness. Worded another way, only the man that she is married to should see her unclothed, and only that man should have a sexual relationship with her. This being the case, if any man has a sexual relationship with his father's wife, then he has uncovered his father's nakedness. So if Ham had a sexual relationship with his father, Noah's wife, he would then have 'seen' the nakedness of Noah or 'uncovered' Noah's nakedness'. Uncovering removes the veil or shield that allows any object to be seen or viewed. This incestuous sin was abhorred by God, and there was a price to pay for such an act.

Leviticus 18:8 KJV

> [8] The nakedness of thy father's wife shalt thou not uncover: it is thy father's nakedness.

When the bible then states that Ham **"saw the nakedness of his father"**, it is saying that he slept with his father's wife. Many have erroneously deduced from Genesis 9:20-27 that Ham committed some sort of same-sex act with Noah, and as a result of this, Ham was cursed with blackness. But let me tell you this, BLACKNESS IS A BLESSING AND NOT A CURSE! Being black gives us a direct link to the very first man who, as we have previously shown, was created as a black man from the earth. Black people should wear their blackness with pride and know that when others discriminate against, oppress, or oppose us on the basis of our skin color, they are actually opposing the God who created us in His image.

So the act of 'uncovering' a father's nakedness as defined in Leviticus fits the narrative of Genesis 9:20-17. Noah, after a long days work in the field, comes home with the intention of going in and having sex with his wife. He starts drinking, gets drunk, and goes in to his wife. But as many drunkards do when they are inebriated, before he could have sex with his wife, he falls asleep. Ham happens to be passing by the tent and sees that his father's wife is undressed; but his father is undressed and asleep. So Ham goes in and does with Noah's wife what Noah had planned to do; and in so doing, he 'uncovered his father's nakedness'. When Noah sobered up and realized what Ham had done, he cursed Canaan. But why Canaan? Because it is widely held that Canaan was the offspring of Ham's ungodly act. It could have been months or even years before Noah realized what had occurred, but when he did, he cursed Canaan. It is generally believed that Canaan was cursed because he was conceived when Ham uncovered his father's nakedness. Or in other words, Canaan was the child of Ham and Noah's wife. The curse was that Canaan would serve Japheth. The wording here lends one to believe that the enlargement of Japheth would be by invading and taking control of the land that was purposed to Canaan and forcing Canaan into indentured servitude. Chattel slavery is cruel and inhumane. God never intended for any of His creation to be the 'property' of another. But the punishment spoken of in the curse of Canaan was that they would become the indentured servants of Japheth. Or, in today's vernacular, they would not be the business owners as their cousins were, but rather they would be the employees of the business.

I shall take this time to also emphasize that slavery of any type today is cruel, inhumane, unrighteous, and not sanctioned or supported by God. There once was a time when God allowed groups to make other groups their servants. These servants were simply workers who were treated like family by their employers. Sometimes they worked to pay off debt; sometimes they were workers because their land had been invaded and taken over by another nation, and sometimes their servitude was a result of their disobedience. Canaan was subjected to punishment for an act that his father committed. Later, when Israel complained about being punished for acts committed by their ancestors, God stopped disciplining children for the acts of their parents.[xxix] Today God emphasizes that there is no different in people[xxx], we are all the same before Him so no one has the right to enslave another human.

The price paid for the act of Ham was that Canaan would lose their heritage to Japheth. But this has no direct bearing on the Cushite, also known as the Ethiopians and Africans.

Looking back at the map of the lands where Ham's sons are indigenous and native to, you see that Mizraim, Put, and Cush are on the African continent whereas Canaan is north of Africa in the Mesopotamia, closer to Asia. I make mention of this because there is no indication that the indigenous black people on the continent of Africa were ever cursed. God never intended for the indigenous black people of Africa to serve anyone as indentured servants or slaves. It is for this reason that black people will fight to our death for freedom and justice. We cannot be indentured servants, we cannot be chattel slaves, nor can we be beholden to anyone because this is not God's will for us, neither is it his way. This is also why indigenous Africans, or black people, would rather perish violently while fighting for freedom than to exist peacefully in unjust submission.

African Americans are descendants of Ham through Cush (Ethiopia), so this curse on Canaan has no direct bearing on us; nor does it have any bearing on our current conditions. We will see that when we examine the bible, Ham's seed, including his offspring through Cush, is called by God for a specific purpose, strategically placed upon this earth, and tremendously favored by God.

Black People are God's People

"Are ye not as children of the **Ethiopian**s unto me, O children of Israel? saith the LORD. Have not I brought up Israel out of the land of Egypt? and the Philistines from Caphtor, and the Syrians from Kir?"[xxxi]

I live in Chicago, Illinois. Chicago is a pretty active sports city. The people of Chicago have a love for sports. They are, for the most part, die-hard sports fans. Now, what if I told you that the Bears are Chicago's team? If you are knowledgeable of sports, me saying that the Bears are 'Chicago's team wouldn't generate any alarm in you. As a matter of fact, you'd probably nod your head in agreement with me. But then what if I told you that the Yankees are coming to Chicago to compete in a game against the Bears? Now, if you are knowledgeable of sports, this would immediately raise a flag! A game between these two teams is not possible because the Yankees are a New York Baseball team and the Bears, although they are 'Chicago's team, they are NOT Chicago's baseball's team. If the Yankees are to play Chicago's team, it has to be a competition against one of Chicago's teams for baseball. Therefore, the Bears cannot be specified merely as Chicago's team. Chicago has many teams. There are the Cubs, the White Sox, the Bulls, and the Black Hawks; all are professional sports teams in Chicago. Each of these teams compete in different sports. So when I say 'The Bears are Chicago's team', because I know the purpose of each of the various teams in Chicago, what I am really saying is 'the Bears are Chicago's team for football', or in other words, 'the Bears are Chicago's football team'. The Cubs, the White Sox, the Bulls, and the Black Hawks are as much Chicago's team as the Bears; they just have different missions, different purposes, and compete in different sports. So to simply say, 'the Bears are Chicago's team' without clarification would not be correct.

Jeremiah 32: 27 KJV

> ²⁷ Behold, I am the Lord, the God of all flesh…

Ezekiel 18:4 KJV

> ⁴ Behold, all souls are mine; as the soul of the father, so also the soul of the son is mine: the soul that sinneth, it shall die.

So to identify any single race or ethnic group as 'God's People' without clarifying and specifying their call, assignment, mission, or purpose is no more correct than when we earlier declared that the Bears are Chicago's team for competitive sports. Since God has declared that all people are His, then when we specify a group of people as God's people, we must also specify the mission, assignment, call, or purpose that God has chosen those people for because God selects specific individuals, groups, people, etc. for specific purposes of work.

Ephesians 4:11 KJV

> ¹¹ And He gave some Apostle, some Prophets, some Evangelists, and some Pastors and Teachers…

This reference from Ephesians shows us that even at the individual level, God selects specific people for specific purposes. And when God selects an individual and assigns them a specific purpose or work, it does not mean that ONLY this individual belongs to God, it simply means that God has selected this individual for a specific work. Are only Apostles, Prophets, Evangelists, Pastors and Teachers God's people?[xxxii] NO! The believers sitting in the pews are as much God's people as any of the people called to the ministerial callings listed in Ephesians 4:11, they just don't have the same assignment, mission, or purpose as those selected for either of the fives functions listed. The apostle Paul rhetorically asked, Are all Apostles? Do all prophesy?[xxxiii]

God also selects groups for specific purposes. Of the twelve tribes or Israel, the tribe of Levi was selected by God to represent Him as His priests among the other tribes.[xxxiv] Does this selection of Levi for the Priestly purpose make them God's ONLY people? No! The other eleven tribes were as much God's people as the tribe of Levi, they just did not have the same assignment, mission, and purpose as Levi.

God even selects entire nations for specific missions and purposes. Abraham was mentioned as the father of a nation (Israel), and God went on to say that through this nation the entire world would be blessed. Genesis 12:2-3 reads

> ² And I will make of thee a great nation, and I will bless thee, and make thy name great; and thou shalt be a blessing:
>
> ³ And I will bless them that bless thee, and curse him that curseth thee: and in thee shall all families of the earth be blessed.

So once Abraham's seed had developed into a nation, God specified to them their assignment, mission, and responsibility on this earth and clearly stated what they were called to do.

Exodus 19:5-6 KJV

> [5] Now therefore, if ye will obey my voice indeed, and keep my covenant, then ye shall be a peculiar treasure unto me above all people: for all the earth is mine:

> [6] And ye shall be unto me a kingdom of priests, and an holy nation. These are the words which thou shalt speak unto the children of Israel.

WOW, WHAT A CALL! Israel was selected by God for the purpose of being His priests among His people. And as awesome as this selection is, and with the tremendous responsibility that it entails, THIS DOES NOT MEAN THAT ISRAEL IS GOD'S ONLY PEOPLE. It simply declares that God has selected Israel for a specific mission and purpose (to be the priests) among all of His people. This is a mission and purpose that is specific to the nation of Israel, and only Israel can fulfill this mission. The bible makes it very clear that Israel's assignment, function, and purpose are to represent God as His Priests among the rest of God's people in the world.

Since Israel is called to be God's Priests to the other nations on the earth, and the bible is God's word to the other nations on the earth, it stands to reason that the bible would document much more information about Israel, the nation selected by God to deliver His message to the rest of His people, than the other nations because, in documenting the **process** of sharing God's word to the world, the bible has to follow the nation (Israel) that has been tasked with the responsibility of delivering this word. THIS IS THEIR PRIESTLY RESPONSIBILITY! And this is the primary reason that the bible provides a very clear and detailed account of who Israel is, as well as what their call and purpose in this world should be. This does not in any way imply that Israel is God's **only** chosen people. They were chosen to be the Priests and to represent God to the other nations, but through Bible study and application, we can extrapolate the function that God selected for and assigned to Ham's descendants (black people).

The mission of the descendants of Ham and their purpose are not as clearly outlined in the bible as the mission and purpose of the Israelites since they were not assigned the Priestly function as Israel was. Therefore, the bible does not closely follow them in their mission as it does Israel. This is largely due to the fact that the bible is God's word to the entire world, and this word was first to be delivered by God to Israel, the descendants of Shem, who is then commanded to carry this word to the world. So, as previously stated, there would be more direct information about Israel recorded in the bible simply because, in order to tell the story of the process of taking God's word to the world, you have to follow the nation/people who were given the responsibility of taking this word to the world.

We can, however, use multiple scriptures and many pertinent points to identify God's assignment to the descendants of Ham (Africans). First, we must consider that the bible clearly shows us that God's relationship with Ham's descendants (Africans) predated His relationship with Shem's Descendants (Israel).

Amos 9:7 KJV

> "⁷Are ye not as children of the **Ethiopian**s unto me, O children of Israel? saith the LORD. Have not I brought up Israel out of the land of Egypt? ..."

Here God specifically says to the children of Abraham (Israel) that they are as dear to Him as the 'children of the Ethiopians'. Then God provides historical detail about some of the things that He did for Israel that validates this statement and proves that they are as dear to Him as the Ethiopians. God is telling Israel that His relationship with the 'Ethiopians' has served as the 'standard' for His relationship with them. God first performed mighty and wondrous works for the Ethiopians, and then He performed similar mighty and wondrous works for the Israelites. This particular verse of scripture itself provides powerful validation of the historical longevity of God's relationship with black people in that we see that God's relationship with black people of African descent, (**Children of the Ethiopians**), pre-dated His relationship with the Jews.

Let's revisit the word 'Ethiopia'. Remember the word Ethiopia is itself a Greek word that mean "BURNT FACE". So although Ethiopia is a nation on the continent of Africa, in the bible the word 'Ethiopians' is used to identify all black people… or in other words, **The indigenous Africans.** We have seen Ethiopia on the previous maps but it is timely to take a quick look again.

This is in no way an attempt to denigrate, disparage, malign, or minimize the importance of Israel as a nation; nor can we ever ignore their ministry or place in this world in respect to God's call. We are simply demonstrating through biblical reference that God has a long-standing relationship with Black people. He gave enormous responsibility to Ham's seed (indigenous Africans and those of African descent) and we are dear to God and have been dear to God throughout the ages.

Some black people have taken to identifying themselves as 'Black Hebrew' or 'Black Jews. They apparently do this to mark themselves as God's people. I will not dispute with them if they want to identify themselves as Jews for this purpose. But I must make two pertinent points that are biblically validated in this book.

1. The Jews are not God's ONLY people. But as earlier stated, they are the people that God selected to be His priests to the world. God has declared that all people are His people.
2. God was in relationship with the Ethiopians (indigenous black Africans) long before He came into relationship with Abraham or his descendants, the Jews. So being a 'Black Hebrew' or 'Black Jew' means that God patterned His relationship with you after the relationship that He already had with the Ethiopians.

According to Amos 9:7, when God called Israel up out of the land of Egypt, and delivered them multiple times, God was showing them that they were as 'dear' to Him as Black People (Children of the Ethiopians). This literally means that whether you are a 'Black Hebrew', a 'White Hebrew', a 'Brown Hebrew', a 'Red Hebrew', or a Hebrew of any color, whatever you claim that God did for you, GOD SAID THAT HE WAS DOING THIS TO SHOW YOU THAT HE CARED AS MUCH FOR YOU AS HE DOES FOR BLACK PEOPLE (CHILDREN OF THE ETHIOPIANS) !

God wanted there to be no doubt about His relationship with Ham's descendants, or as we know them, the indigenous Black people of Africa; nor did God want any doubt to exist regarding their prominence in His plan for the world.

Psalms 68:31 KJV

> [31] Princes shall come out of Egypt; Ethiopia shall soon stretch out her hands unto God.

Our next step in identifying God's assigned responsibility for the descendants of Ham is to examine their function as recorded in the bible. When doing this, we see that God always sent His Priests (Israel) to the land of Ham (Africa) when they needed assistance, nurturing, provision, or protection. Africans provided assistance, nurture, and protection to the Jews, starting with Abraham and continuing throughout the bible. Immediately after God called Abram, He sent him to Africa so that the Africans could provide, nurture, protect, & sustain him during a time of famine.

Genesis 12:10 KJV

> ¹⁰ And there was a famine in the land: and Abram went down into Egypt to sojourn there; for the famine was grievous in the land.

At the time God sent Abram into Egypt (Africa), God knew that He would call Israel to be His priests upon this earth. And as dear as Abram was to Him, and as critical to this world as the future responsibilities of Israel would be, by sending Abraham to Africa for his provision, protection, and support, God demonstrated confidence and faith in Ham's descendants that they would do right by him, take care of him, provide for him, protect him, and nurture him. This they did because of their relationship with God, and it was the Godly thing to do!

Abraham's Descent From His Father's House Into Africa (Egypt)

When studying the bible, you should always keep in mind that, as earlier stated, Egypt and Libya are on the continent of Africa. That makes Egyptians and Libyans the offspring of Ham and indigenous Africans. There had to be a very strong bond between God and the Africans. So strong that God trusted them to nurture and sustain Abraham, whose seed had been selected to serve as His priests to all the other nations of the world and thereby cause the entire world to be blessed. The very fact that God had such confidence in the Africans at this critical time speaks to the bond that existed between God and the Africans. However, this was not the only time that the bible records the fact that God sent His priests (Israel) to Africa for protection and sustenance; it was merely the first time. Consider what God did two generations later when Jacob was faced with the same problem of famine as his grandfather Abraham.

Genesis 46:5-6 KJV

> ⁵ And Jacob rose up from Beersheba: and the sons of Israel carried Jacob their father, and their little ones, and their wives, in the wagons which Pharaoh had sent to carry him.

> ⁶ And they took their cattle, and their goods, which they had gotten in the land of Canaan, and came into Egypt, Jacob, and all his seed with him:

Here, as with Abraham earlier, God sends Jacob and His sons to Africa so that the Africans can protect and sustain them during a great famine. But as we know from bible study, this time the African nation of Egypt has the responsibility to nurture them as they increased in population from Jacob and his sons into a nation of people.

Psalms 105:23 KJV

> ²³Israel also came into Egypt; and Jacob sojourned in the land of Ham.

These incidents show the African Nation of Egypt providing assistance, nurture, and protection to Israel. But Egypt is not the only descendant of Ham that the bible records as providing assistance and protection to Israel during their trying times.

2 Kings 19:6-9 KJV

> [6] And Isaiah said unto them, Thus shall ye say to your master, Thus saith the LORD, Be not afraid of the words which thou hast heard, with which the servants of the king of Assyria have blasphemed me.
>
> [7] Behold, I will send a blast upon him, and he shall hear a rumour, and shall return to his own land; and I will cause him to fall by the sword in his own land.
>
> [8] So Rabshakeh returned, and found the king of Assyria warring against Libnah: for he had heard that he was departed from Lachish.
>
> [9] And when he heard say of Tirhakah king of Ethiopia, Behold, he is come out to fight against thee: he sent messengers again unto Hezekiah, saying,

The above scripture reference from 2 Kings records an account of Israel facing sure defeat at the hands of a fierce Assyrian King. So powerful and mighty was this opposition that fear set upon the Israelites. But God sent word via the prophet Isaiah that they should not fear because He would send deliverance that would be a 'blast' upon the Assyrian king and his army. From whence did this deliverance come?

From Tirhakah, the king of Ethiopia, and his Ethiopian army. African assistance to Israel and support of Israel during their trying times is well documented in the bible. When Herod, a descendant of Japheth, sought to murder the child Jesus, God once again sent His son, the savior of the world, into Africa for protection and support. We will re-visit this incident later as we discuss the skin color of Jesus.

Matthew 2:13-15 KJV

> [13] And when they were departed, behold, the angel of the Lord appeareth to Joseph in a dream, saying, Arise, and take the young child and his mother, and flee into Egypt, and be thou there until I bring thee word: for Herod will seek the young child to destroy him.

> [14] When he arose, he took the young child and his mother by night, and departed into Egypt:

> [15] And was there until the death of Herod: that it might be fulfilled which was spoken of the Lord by the prophet, saying, Out of Egypt have I called my son.

Even as the Romans, who are also descendants of Japheth, are marching our Lord and Savior to the crucifixion, once again it was an African from Cyrene, a city in Libya, who was 'compelled' to help Jesus.

Mark 15:21 KJV

> ²¹ And they compel one Simon a Cyrenian, who passed by, coming out of the country, the father of Alexander and Rufus, to bear his cross.

We see time and time again that when Israel needed assistance, nurturing, and protection, God sent the seed of Ham, or the Africans, to provide this aid. So when considering the totality of these recorded incidents and the duties that God called upon the Africans to perform, we can see time and time again that when Israel needed assistance, nurturing, and protection, God sent the seed of Ham, or the Africans, to provide this aid. So when considering the totality of these recorded incidents and the duties that God called upon the Africans to perform, we can see that God's assignment, purpose, and call for Black People, or the seed of Ham, is to support, protect, and nurture God's righteousness, His sacred priests, and all that He has set aside and declared Holy. This would be one of the primary reasons the world always has better harmony when Israel is in partnership with Africa. Both Africa and Israel are called by God and have very defined responsibilities within God's plan for the world. Israel's assignment from God is identified by the commandment from God to them, as shown earlier, whereas Ham's descendants (Black People) assignment from God is identified by the function that God tasked them with.

Now some will wonder whether it is appropriate to extrapolate God's call for Black people by analyzing the biblical functions assigned to them by God. But this is consistent with bible teaching in other areas. Just consider the very angels. Nowhere in the bible does it ever state that Gabriel is an Archangel or that he is God's messenger angel. But through consistent and methodical bible study, we have extrapolated Gabriel's call by looking at the work that God assigned to him. Whenever we read of Gabriel in the bible, he is delivering messages from God[xxxv] ; therefore, we can determine that Gabriel was created by God to be His messenger.

And since we know of the rank of Michael, we acknowledge that Gabriel too must be an Archangel because of his critical responsibility.

Likewise, we can extrapolate that Michael is God's fighting angel because whenever the bible speaks of him, he is representing God either fighting the forces of evil himself or leading an Army of angels against the forces of evil[xxxvi]. Therefore, we have determined that Michael was created by God to be His warring Angel.

This same bible study concept would remain true for black people who are the descendants of Ham. We have seen the duties that God consistently called upon the Africans to perform, so from these duties, we can determine that God's assignment for the descendants of Ham, as utilized by God and documented in the bible, is to be the <u>protectors</u>

and <u>nurturers of what's Godly and righteous</u>. God equipped Ham's descendants (Black People) with the STRENGTH, POWER, WEALTH, INTELLECT, WISDOM, and MIGHT to successfully fulfill their assigned mission in every aspect of life.

We have seen thus far that God has a long, rich, and committed relationship with Ham's descendants. Many find this hard to believe, primarily because of the way Africans have been erroneously portrayed in movies or written about in mainstream media. But we should keep in mind that those presenting the nations on the African continent, whether through film or in writings, have much to gain by falsely presenting the indigenous African people as poor, unlearned, unstructured, and unorganized idol-worshipping savages. But the reality is that any presentation of Africans in this manner is NOT TRUE! It is exactly the opposite of who Africans really are! Historical and biblical Africans displayed all the intellect, wealth, health, power, and might that are inherent in any people that have God's favor upon them. This is what we know about the historical and biblical Africans, they were:

- Blessed (The vast wealth of the world (gold, oil, Onyx, silicon, platinum, etc.) was given to them by God when he gave them Africa as their land)
- Brilliant (The great Pyramids are engineering marvels even to this day and they instituted embalming of the dead with the process known as mummifying)

- Resourceful (When the earth was afflicted with famine, they were resourceful enough to not only survive, but assist others in surviving)
- Wealthy (Throughout the bible, you read of the wealth Africans such as the Queen of Sheba and other Africans)
- Spiritual (They understood that their existence was not because of themselves, so they sought someone or something to worship and give credit for life. They also expected another life after earthly death)

These things are all indications of the blessings and favor of God upon any people with whom God has a positive relationship. As a matter of fact, Ham's descendants were known for their abundance and blessings as a result of their relationship with God.

1 Chronicles 4:40 KJV

> ^{40} And they found fat pasture and good, and the land was wide, and quiet, and peaceable; for they of Ham had dwelt there of old.

Note that the land was described as wide, quiet, and peaceable because "THEY OF HAM HAD DWELT THERE OF OLD". This land was blessed and the blessings that were upon it are directly related to the fact that BLACK PEOPLE (Ham's descendants) lived there. God always honor commitment and dedication to Him, His will, and His way.

Proverbs 10:22 KJV

> ²²The blessing of the Lord, it maketh rich…

The previous listing of what we know about biblical Africans well demonstrates that the blessings of God were upon Ham and his descendants. However, it is the "SPIRITUAL" characteristic that I will elaborate on.

One of the hardest things for many people, including black people, to understand is that Ham's seed **ALWAYS** served the **true** and **living God**, even before Israel existed. AFRICANS NEVER WORSHIPPED IDOL GODS! As previously stated, the Black descendants of Ham in biblical times were brilliant people, and they knew that they were not responsible for their existence. They understood that a higher authority and power were responsible for their existence, and this power controlled the natural processes of the world altogether. This they realized by being aware and knowledgeable of their surroundings. In Romans 1:20, the Apostle Paul worded it this way…

Romans 1:20 KJV

> ²⁰ For the invisible things of him from the creation of the world are clearly seen, being understood by the things that are made, even his eternal power and Godhead;

Biblical Africans understood the existence of a higher supreme power because they could clearly see the invisible things of Him from the creation of the world. What made them brilliant is that they then acknowledged and accepted that they did not create the world, nor could they control such things as the sun, the moon, the wind, the rain, seasons, etc. But their acknowledging and accepting this fact is only one facet of their brilliance. The primary indication of their brilliance is that once they acknowledged the existence of a Supreme Being and accepted that this Supreme Being was responsible for these great, mighty, and powerful wonders, they then sought to serve and worship this Supreme Being. So with the understanding that they owed their existence to this Supreme Being, but without knowledge of who this Supreme Being was, biblical Africans still expressed gratitude to this Supreme Being through worship. This they did by creating images of Gold, Silver, and other precious materials, which they used to symbolize the Supreme Being of whom they had no knowledge. In other words,

They were worshiping God without knowledge of God!

They were not worshipping these images of gold, silver, or stone that they created with their hands, but they were using these images as a representation of the Supreme Being that today we know is God.

But can one worship and serve a God for whom they have no knowledge? The Apostle Paul indicated that some in Athens were doing just this.

Acts 17:23 KJV

> ²³ For as I passed by, and beheld your devotions, I found an altar with this inscription, To The Unknown God. Whom therefore ye ignorantly worship, Him declare I unto you.

Jesus said to the Samaritan woman at the well that her people did not know who they worshipped, but the Jews knew because God had revealed Himself to Them.

John 4:22 KJV

> ²² Ye worship ye know not what: we know what we worship: for salvation is of the Jews.

So, biblical Africans were worshipping God without knowledge of who God was. And in doing this, they created images of wood, gold, silver, etc., to represent the God of whom they had no knowledge. And God, being just, understood that they had no knowledge of Him and that these created images were being used to represent Him, overlooked their acts, and accounted it for what it was, ignorance of God. This is how the bible states that God dealt with them.

Acts 17:29-30 KJV

> ²⁹ Forasmuch then as we are the offspring of God, we ought not to think that the Godhead is like unto gold, or silver, or stone, graven by art and man's device.

> ³⁰ And the times of this ignorance God winked at;
> but now commandeth all men everywhere to repent:

When Ham's descendants had no knowledge of who God was, God overlooked the making of gold, silver, and stone images used to represent Him. It was not that they were not serving and worshipping God, because they were. As humans, they needed something to represent God to them, and they found this in their created images. And how did God respond to the making of these images of gold, silver, stone, etc., to represent Him? HE WINKED AT IT! In other words, God <u>overlooked</u> their ignorance at the time. But today, when knowledge of Him abounds, God no longer winks but requires repentance of all men everywhere. It was the job of Israel, as the nation that was called to be God's priests upon this earth, first to acquire knowledge of God, then distribute this knowledge throughout the world, thereby bringing a blessing upon the entire world. It was not unusual for Ham's seed to be without knowledge of God at that time because even the nation that God called to be His priests (Israel) had no knowledge of Him. While in Egypt, they too were calling on the Supreme Being that they did not know. This we know because when Moses was commanded to go to them, he asked God who should he say sent him and, in whose name, should he say he has come. Moses specifically tells God that his Hebrew kin people don't know who you are.[xxxvii] And God said to Moses, just tell them I AM hath sent you.

So Israel had these three responsibilities in regards to serving as God's priests to the world;

1. They had to acquire knowledge of God for themselves.
2. They were to make God known unto the descendants of Ham so that they would no longer serve Him without knowledge of who He was.
3. They were to bring the Gentiles, (the descendants of Japheth), into fellowship with God.

So once knowledge of God became available, God no longer 'winked' at this ignorance but rather called upon all men everywhere to repent. Since the unveiling of God, knowledge of God has permeated the African continent.

The Bible reveals multiple instances where the ethical, just, and moral decisions of Africans showed character that is consistent with people in relationship with God. The African people had such a sincere relationship with God that when God determined that Israel had developed into a nation and were ready to depart from Egypt, He had to 'raise up' a king in Egypt with a hardened heart that was willing to mistreat the Israeli people.[xxxviii]

The following incidents provide insight into the Godly character of the African Kings and the African people. Their Godly character can be seen by the way in which they interacted with Abraham, Joseph, Jacob, and Israel.

- Note how the King of Egypt treated Abram and Sarah in Genesis chapter 12. According to verses 12-20, Pharaoh's character in this incident was the character of one that feared God, and walked in the ways of God, even though at this time they had no DIRECT knowledge of God. He even became angered when he realized that Abram said Sarah was his sister.
- Note how the King of Egypt treated Joseph and his entire family, thus saving Israel from sure death then nurturing Israel into a nation. (Genesis 39)
- Note how Tirhakah king of Ethiopia, came to Israel's aid when the King of Assyria was set to destroy Jerusalem… (2 Kings 19)
- Even note how Simon of Cyrene did not push back when compelled to carry the cross of Jesus… (Mark 15:21)

It is clear that the descendants of Shem (Israel) assignment & duty is to represent God as priests and introduce God to the entire world. In contrast, scripture shows that the assignment and duty of Ham's descendants (Africans & those of African Descent) is to protect & nurture God's righteousness (Israel) in the earth.

God's relationship with the descendants of Ham (**Black People**) is based on Trust. As we have seen, God trusted the indigenous Africans to look after and protect Abraham, Israel, and even Jesus in their most pressing and vulnerable times. He knew that any people who would serve Him without direct knowledge of Him, which Ham's descendants did, could be trusted! And once God places that level of trust in a nation and assigns such responsibility upon a nation or people, He does not repent for it.[xxxix]

Earlier we stated that the bible provides more information about the Jews than it does about the descendants of Ham simply because they are called to be God's priests. As such, they were responsible for receiving knowledge and instruction from God, then sharing this with the world. So naturally, there would be more documented information in the bible about them because the writer of the written record would have to follow them as they performed their ministerial duties as priests. But that is not to say that Ham's seeds aren't mentioned because they are. And each time that they are mentioned, they are shown to have ethical and Godly character while making morally just decisions. The bible mentions Africans as Kings, Queens, Princes, Women of Beauty, Men of Strength, Smart, Knowledge Seekers, etc. I will close this book by highlighting a few of the prominent black people mentioned in the Bible, but first, let's perform a brief synopsis/survey of the Old Testament relative to all of the descendants of Noah's three sons.

HENRY L. RAZOR

A Very Brief Synopsis of God's Assignment to All Mankind Through Insight of The Old Testament

As I conclude this chapter I must pause and add clarity to the premise of this book, relative to the Holy Scriptures. One of the most deceptive, hocus-pocus, sleight-of-hand tactics that has ever been taught to black people, the black church, and indigenous Africans in general, is that someone, at some point in history, convinced black religious leaders that black people are Gentiles. And this lie has been passed down through generations in our churches without challenge or without even applying the truth of the scriptures to it. But we have shown that the Gentiles are descendants of Japheth. (Genesis 10:2-5).

> *2. The sons of Japheth; Gomer, and Magog, and Madai, and Javan, and Tubal, and Meshech, and Tiras.*
>
> *3. And the sons of Gomer; Ashkenaz, and Riphath, and Togarmah.*
>
> *4. And the sons of Javan; Elishah, and Tarshish, Kittim, and Dodanim.*
>
> *5. By these were the isles of the Gentiles divided in their lands; every one after his tongue, after their families, in their nations.*

Black people are descendants of Ham as previously stated in this book.

So the basis for this lie has always been that the Bible only mentions two classes or groups of people, the Jews and the

Gentiles. Therefore, if you are not a Jew, then you must be a Gentile. But Noah had three sons, not two. Therefore, this lie could never be true, has never been true, and will never be true.

We see in Genesis chapter 9:18-19, that God makes it very clear that the entire world comes from Noah's three sons.

> *18. And the sons of Noah, that went forth of the ark, were Shem, and Ham, and Japheth: and Ham is the father of Canaan.*
>
> *19. These are the three sons of Noah: and of them was the whole earth overspread.*

That's correct, THREE sons, not two. We've already shown that the Jews came from Shem, the Africans came from Ham, and the Caucasians came from Japheth. So to say that the Bible only speaks of two groups of people is factually incorrect. Your understanding of the Bible will greatly increase when you understand the assignment of God for all three of these groups. I have already taken the time to provide the detail in the previous pages of this book, but for clarity, I will provide a synopsis of these three groups, relative to God. This synopsis will prove to be a great aid in studying the Bible.

The Bible is God's word that lays out His will for the human race (mankind). So when reading and studying, we will have a better understanding if we keep the following in mind.

- God is the creator of all things.

- He is the ruler of this universe and every universe that is unknown to man
- He is the Supreme Being.

The inhabitants of the world as we know it today emanated from Noah's three sons. Initially, all of Noah's sons knew God as the Supreme Being. They recognized God as the creator that is above all. However, none of Noah's descendants initially knew God **as God**; they only knew that an all-powerful Supreme Being created the earth and everything that is in it. The descendants of Shem and the descendants of Ham reverenced this Supreme Being and gave honor to Him through various methods (Acts 17:29-30). However, the descendants of Japheth dismissed this Supreme Being and went forth in the world in their power and authority.

SHEM AND HIS DESCENDANTS

We have biblical evidence that the descendants of Shem were honoring this Supreme Being even prior to knowing Him as Yahweh, Jehovah, Elohim, Allah, or God. When Moses was sent to Africa to bring the Israelites out, He said to God that they don't know you by your name. Exodus 3:13-15 reads:

> *13. And Moses said unto God, Behold, when I come unto the children of Israel, and shall say unto them, The God of your fathers hath sent me unto you; and they shall say to me, What is his name? what shall I say unto them?*
>
> *14. And God said unto Moses, I AM THAT I AM: and he said, Thus shalt thou say unto the children of Israel, I AM hath sent me unto you.*

> *15. And God said moreover unto Moses, Thus shalt thou say unto the children of Israel, The LORD God of your fathers, the God of Abraham, the God of Isaac, and the God of Jacob, hath sent me unto you: this is my name for ever, and this is my memorial unto all generations.*

God selected these Descendants of Shem (the Jews) to be his priests to all human kind. This assignment was made to the Jews by commandment of God. Exodus 19:4-6 reads

> *4. ye have seen what I did unto the Egyptians, and how I bare you on eagles' wings, and brought you unto myself.*
>
> *5. Now therefore, if ye will obey my voice indeed, and keep my covenant, then ye shall be a peculiar treasure unto me above all people: for all the earth is mine:*
>
> *6. and ye shall be unto me a kingdom of priests, and an holy nation. These are the words which thou shalt speak unto the children of Israel.*

In order to function as His priests, God had to first reveal Himself to them, provide them with knowledge of Him, then send them out with His message.

HAM AND HIS DESCENDANTS

> The descendants of Ham were also reverencing and worshipping the Supreme creator without knowing Him by name.
>
> We have biblical evidence that the descendants of Ham were honoring this Supreme Being even prior to knowing Him as Yahweh, Jehovah, Elohim,

Allah, or God. This evidence is validated by God's trust in them when calling, developing, and commissioning the Jews as his priests. God fully trusted the descendants of Ham, as evidenced by selecting them to provide support for Abraham, thus preserving his life. Genesis 12:10 reads:

> **10. And there was a famine in the land: and Abram went down into Egypt to sojourn there; for the famine was grievous in the land.**

I love referencing the above scripture because I find even more compelling evidence that the descendants of Ham reverenced the Supreme Being by observing the ethical and moral way that Pharaoh reacted when he learned that Sarai was Abraham's wife and not his sister. (Genesis 12:14-20)

We also see God's trust in the descendants of Ham was so great that He sent Jacob there so that the descendants of Ham or the '*Hamites*' in Africa could nurture and protect them as God developed them into a great nation. Exodus 1:1-7 reads

1. Now these are the names of the children of Israel, which came into Egypt; every man and his household came with Jacob.

2. Reuben, Simeon, Levi, and Judah,

3. Issachar, Zebulun, and Benjamin,

> *4. Dan, and Naphtali, Gad, and Asher.*
>
> *5. And all the souls that came out of the loins of Jacob were seventy souls: for Joseph was in Egypt already.*
>
> *6. And Joseph died, and all his brethren, and all that generation.*
>
> *7. And the children of Israel were fruitful, and increased abundantly, and multiplied, and waxed exceeding mighty; and the land was filled with them.*

We also see that God sent King Tirhakah from Ethiopia to deliver His priests when they were sure to be wiped out by the powerful Assyrian King. 2 Kings 19:8-9 reads:

> *[8] So Rabshakeh returned, and found the king of Assyria warring against Libnah: for he had heard that he was departed from Lachish.*
>
> *[9] And when he heard say of Tirhakah king of Ethiopia, Behold, he is come out to fight against thee: he sent messengers again unto Hezekiah, saying,*

These are but a few of the instances in the Bible where the descendants of Ham, or the ***Hamites***, were called upon by God to function as the providers, protectors, and nurturers of God's priests and His covenant.

The descendants of Ham were even called upon to protect and provide for Jesus when King Herod sought to take his life. (Matthew 2:13-15).

Throughout the Bible, we see that the descendants of Ham functioned as the nurturers, guardians, and protectors of

God's priests and thereby His covenant. This is a powerful indicator of God's assignment to the descendants of Ham. This assignment as the nurturers, protectors and providers of God's priests and God's covenant was evidenced by the function God selected for them throughout the Bible. Therefore, we see that God's assignment to the descendants of Ham, as evidenced by scripture, is by the function that they provided under the guidance of God.

Even more evidence of God's trust in Ham's descendants and their close relationship with Him prior to knowing Him as God is the blessings of God that were poured into the homeland of the indigenous descendants of Ham. Africa is by far the richest land in the world because God trusted Ham's descendants.

JAPHETH AND HIS DESCENDANTS

However, we find no evidence in the Bible that the descendants of Japheth ever reverenced the Supreme Being as the descendants of Shem and Ham did. All evidence provided in the scriptures indicates that the descendants of Japheth knowingly and willingly rejected God, choosing material gain instead. Paul even indicated that they knew the truth but hid it to gain materially in the world. He even states that when they knew God, they knowingly and willingly decided not to recognize Him as God. Romans 1:18-22 Paul writes;

> *18. For the wrath of God is revealed from heaven against all ungodliness and unrighteousness of men, who hold the truth in unrighteousness;*
>
> *19. because that which may be known of God is manifest in them; for God hath shewed it unto them.*
>
> *20. For the invisible things of him from the creation of the world are clearly seen, being understood by the things that are made, even his eternal power and Godhead; so that they are without excuse:*
>
> *21. because that, when they knew God, they glorified him not as God, neither were thankful; but became vain in their imaginations, and their foolish heart was darkened.*
>
> *22. Professing themselves to be wise, they became fools,*

Paul goes even further when he reveals that the descendants of Japheth sacrificed to devils. 1 Corinthians 10:20 reads:

> *20. But I say, that the things which the Gentiles sacrifice, they sacrifice to devils, and not to God: and I would not that ye should have fellowship with devils.*

Jesus said of descendants of Japheth that they enslaved other people and took dominion over and subdued men. Matthew 20:25-26b reads:

> *25. But Jesus called them unto him, and said, Ye know that the princes of the Gentiles exercise dominion over them, and they that are great exercise authority upon them.*
>
> *26. But it shall not be so among you:*

Paul even advises that those that reverence God should not behave as the descendants of Japheth, because their actions and character indicate that in his day, Japheth's descendants were so far removed from God that they had lost their knowledge of God. 1 Thessalonians 4:3-5 reads:

> ***3. For this is the will of God, even your sanctification, that ye should abstain from fornication:***
>
> ***4. that every one of you should know how to possess his vessel in sanctification and honour;***
>
> ***5. not in the lust of concupiscence, even as the Gentiles which know not God:***

It was, therefore, the mission of God's priests, or the Jews, to first learn of God, then bring the descendants of Japheth, or the Gentiles, back into a relationship with God.

Consequently, since God revealed Himself as God to the Jews first, they had an additional task of making known to the descendants of Ham who God is. This would allow Ham's descendants to cease worshipping God as a Supreme Being and worship Him as who He is, as who He identified Himself to His priests, the Lord God that created all.

Through careful study of the Old Testament and extrapolation of the scriptures, we see that the Jews failed as priests on the earth. This resulted in Ham's descendants, or the indigenous Africans, not acquiring knowledge of God <u>by His name</u>; (***keep in mind that they were already serving God*** *as the Supreme Being), even without knowledge of Him by name. I expounded on this earlier in this book*). This also resulted in the descendants of Japheth, or the Gentiles, remaining out of a relationship with God. Thus they continued to subdue and enslave others, practice perverseness, and violate every law of God for their personal material gain.

So what was the remedy when Shem's descendants failed as the priests to the world?

JESUS!

God sent Jesus! Jesus is the answer!

Notable Black People of
The Bible

"Can the Ethiopian change his skin" xl

Since the Garden of Eden was located in Africa and the first man was created from the dust of Africa, it stands to reason that the vast majority of the people in the bible would be brown-skinned, colored, or black people. But in this book, my focus is specifically on the Black descendants of Ham, or the indigenous Africans, and those of African descent. Let's take a brief look at a few prominent black people mentioned in the bible.

When identifying prominent black people of the bible, we must begin with Jesus. Although Jesus is a descendant of Noah's son Shem, we have shown previously that Ham was pertinent in his lineage. Let's briefly revisit that chart.

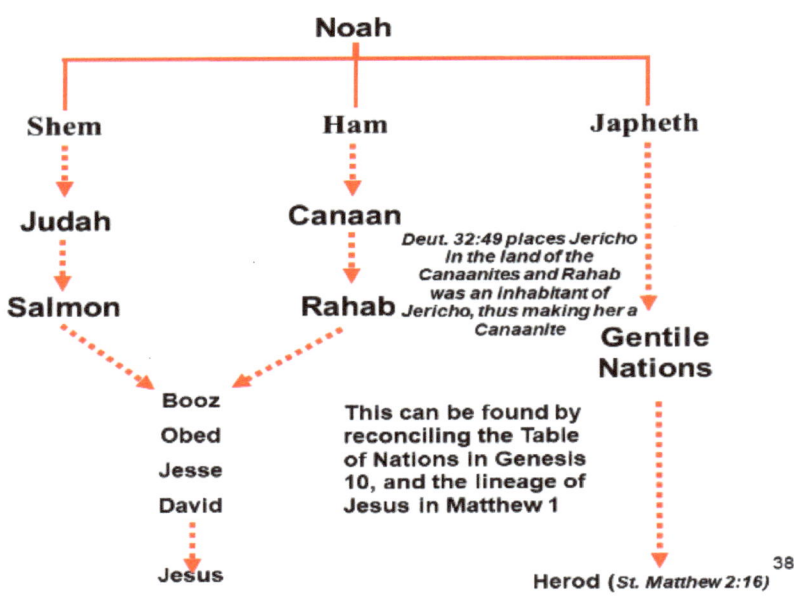

I start with Jesus only because the bible provides unquestionable proof that Jesus was a dark brown-skinned man.

Once again, I call to your remembrance that Noah did not give birth to sons of three colors; neither did he give birth to three races. Noah gave birth to three sons who became three nations. Also, remember the work of Dr. Nina Jablonski, which I mentioned earlier, that variations in human skin are adaptive traits that correlate closely to geography and the sun's ultraviolet radiation. Since Adam and Eve both were black, it would stand to reason that if Noah remained near the land native to Adam and Eve, both he and his sons would retain the traits and skin color of Adam and Eve. It wasn't until Shem and Japheth traveled away from the equator that they adapted to their new environments over time, and their skin color changed to make them suitable for survival in their new environments. So it should not be considered unusual that Jesus also would be dark-skinned, maybe not as dark as Ham's descendants through Cush, but just as dark as Ham's descendants through Mizraim and Put.

Revelations give us the most definitive description of the person of Jesus.

Revelation 1:13-16 KJV

> [13] And in the midst of the seven candlesticks one like unto the Son of man, clothed with a garment down to the foot, and girt about the paps with a golden girdle.

¹⁴ His head and his hairs were white like wool, as white as snow; and his eyes were as a flame of fire;

¹⁵ And his feet like unto fine brass, as if they burned in a furnace; and his voice as the sound of many waters.

¹⁶ And he had in his right hand seven stars: and out of his mouth went a sharp two-edged sword: and his countenance was as the sun shineth in his strength.

I will start with the description of His feet. Verse 15 says his feet were like fine brass. Brass is brown or chocolate. So, according to Revelation 1:14, the skin on Jesus' feet was a bronze color as the color of brass. I have included here a picture depicting a bass shield.

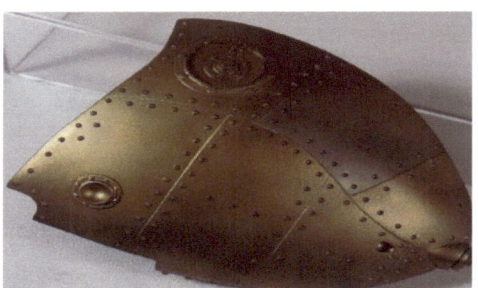

Fine Brass

Now, unless the skin on Jesus' body and face were a different color than the skin on His feet, it is safe to say that his body and face would also be the color of fine brass. Verse 14 further states that His hair was white and His eyes as flames of fire. Putting this physical description together, we get a man that looks very close to the one pictured.

Jesus as Depicted in the Bible

A bronze-skinned Jesus would not be unique among others in the region. Consider how God protected Him when Herod sought to kill Him. God told Joseph to take Him to Egypt and hide Him in that African Nation until Herod died. The bronze-skinned child Jesus would have blended in well with the other Africans of the region simply because He looked like them. They had the same skin color!

You can even perform a little experiment yourself. Try hiding a pink object among brown objects. Then have someone attempt to identify the object you hid; now repeat the experiment, but this time hide a brown object among other brown objects and have someone attempt to identify the object you hid. Now think, if the object you wish to hide is in jeopardy and being pursued. Which situation provides more protection for your object, hiding a pink object among brown objects or hiding a brown object among other brown objects? So by sending Jesus to Africa when Herod sought to kill Him, God was sending Him to a place where he blended in with the other 'bronze skinned' babies in the country, thereby making it even more difficult for Herod to locate and identify Him.

The Queen of Sheba

1 Kings 10:1-2 reads

> [1] And when the queen of Sheba heard of the fame of Solomon concerning the name of the Lord, she came to prove him with hard questions.

> [2] And she came to Jerusalem with a very great train, with camels that bare spices, and very much gold, and precious stones: and when she was come to Solomon, she communed with him of all that was in her heart.

The first time the word "**queen**" is used in the Bible, it refers to a Black woman (1 Kings 10:1). The Scriptures refer to her as the Queen of Sheba or the Queen of the South. Her fame was such that over 2,000 years after her death, Jesus mentioned her long trip and referred to her challenge of Solomon's wisdom[xli], which led to a love affair with the wise Jewish king. But the primary point of the Queen of Sheba's visit is often overlooked. When the queen came to Solomon, she asked him hard questions to see if he would provide correct answers. Once he provided the correct answers, she returned to Africa and told of his wisdom. So what God used this black queen from Africa to do was validate Solomon's wisdom to the rest of the world. Because the queen was brilliant, highly respected, and highly revered, her approval of Solomon would lend credibility to Solomon and lead to Solomon's acceptance by other world leaders. The very fact that Jesus mentions her validation indeed proves the prestige and value of her endorsement.

She was beautiful, rich, smart, and a leader among her people and others. Jesus said that she "came from the utmost parts of the earth to hear the Wisdom of Solomon", so she was a knowledge seeker. She was also a Godly woman that followed after God and obeyed Him. As such, Jesus said that this righteous African queen would rise in judgment against the wicked people of His generation because once God's anointing upon Solomon was made known to her, she traveled a great distance to behold it and experience it.

The Queen of Sheba was Biblically Black and Blessed!

Zipporah (Wife of Moses)

Numbers 12:1 reads

> 12 And Miriam and Aaron spake against Moses because of the Ethiopian woman whom he had married: for he had married an Ethiopian woman.

Moses, who is credited with writing the first five books of the Bible, married an Ethiopian woman, Zipporah, and was persecuted for it. He had to endure direct opposition and persecution because she was African and because of her Ethiopic religious roots. God, Himself, brought judgment because of this African woman.

This had to be a woman of such extraordinary beauty that Moses would look beyond the Hebrew women and set his hearts' desire on her. It is an uncontested fact that black women are some of the most beautiful women in the world! They are smart, strong, loving, faithful, and beautiful.

But when I recall Moses' mission, it is the belief of this author that the ethnic origin of Moses' wife was a part of God's overall plan. Remember that we have already shown that Africans were in a relationship with God before Abraham was called by God. God has always had a special relationship with the Ethiopians or indigenous black people. Also, remember that the Garden of Eden was either in Ethiopia or in close proximity to Ethiopia. God also specifically stated that the children of the Ethiopians were dear to Him and when He delivered Israel from Egypt, He was only doing for them what He had already done for Ethiopia[xlii].

Since the Bible states that a wife is a 'help meet' for her husband, in Moses selection of a wife, we see Black people once again assisting Israel in the deliverance of their nation. Is not this the mission of Black people that we extrapolated from scriptures earlier in this book?

Zipporah was Biblically Black and Blessed!

Nimrod (A Mighty One In The Earth)

Genesis 10:8-10 reads

> [8] And Cush begat Nimrod: he began to be a mighty one in the earth.
>
> [9] He was a mighty hunter before the LORD: wherefore it is said, Even as Nimrod the mighty hunter before the LORD.
>
> [10] And the beginning of his kingdom was Babel, and Erech, and Accad, and Calneh, in the land of Shinar.

Nimrod was Ham's grandson, and he was the first governmental leader, according to the Scripture. The Bible indicates Nimrod was the first king in human history, and he ruled from the location in which he attempted to construct the tower of Babel after the great flood of Noah (Genesis 10:10). The world depended on his hunting expertise to supply food after the flood when animals migrated back to their natural habitats. Genesis refers to Nimrod as a 'mighty hunter' before the Lord.

Many call someone whom they deem as uncultured or silly a Nimrod, and, therefore, they show a severe lack of knowledge of Scripture because we see in Genesis that Nimrod was far from being dumb. Nimrod was a great man in the eyesight of God. He loved God so that he set out to build a tower to Heaven so that he could be close to God.

Many erroneously deem his attempt to build the Tower of Babel to be a rebellion against God. But nowhere in the Bible is this stated or even implied! The fact is that even though God prevented him from building the tower, God commended Nimrod for being a 'mighty one in the earth.' And God at no time condemned Nimrod for his attempt to build the Tower of Babel or for any of his other efforts.

Nimrod was Biblically Black and Blessed!

Tirhakah (King of Ethiopia)

2 Kings 19:8-10 reads

> [8] So Rabshakeh returned, and found the king of Assyria warring against Libnah: for he had heard that he was departed from Lachish.
>
> [9] And when he heard say of Tirhakah king of Ethiopia, Behold, he is come out to fight against thee: he sent messengers again unto Hezekiah, saying,

> [10] Thus shall ye speak to Hezekiah king of Judah, saying, Let not thy God in whom thou trustest deceive thee, saying, Jerusalem shall not be delivered into the hand of the king of Assyria.

Earlier in this book, we mentioned how God sent the king from Ethiopia to be a 'blast' against the Assyrian king when Israel was threatened. King Tirhakah, and the Ethiopian army that he commanded, waged war against Sennacherib during the reign of King Hezekiah of Judah (2 Kings 19:9; Isaiah 37:9) and drove him from his intention of destroying Jerusalem and taking the city's Jewish inhabitants and making them servants[xliii]. God used this African king to protect and support the His covenant and the Jews.

Tirhakah was Biblically Black and Blessed!

Simon of Cyrene

Mark 18:20-21 reads

> [20] And when they had mocked him, they took off the purple from him, and put his own clothes on him, and led him out to crucify him.
>
> [21] And they compel one **Simon a Cyrenian**, who passed by, coming out of the country, the father of Alexander and Rufus, to bear his cross.

The only people that did not willingly participate in the murder of Jesus were Blacks. That's right! Shem's descendants lied on Jesus and falsely convicted Him and sentenced Him to die. Japheth's descendants carried out the crucifixion, thereby committing an act of capital murder against an innocent man. However, Ham's descendants refused to join in as a conspirator in this evil act. But Simon of Cyrene, a descendant of Ham, had the cross of the Son of God forcefully placed on his back by a Roman guard and he had to carry the cross of "human redemption" the rest of the way to the crucifixion.

Even with his forced participation, Simon of Cyrene was completing the assignment of God to the descendants of Ham and fulfilling the call of God to indigenous black people by assisting Jesus. He was doing what Ham's descendants (Egyptian Africans) had done for Abraham; he was doing what Ham's descendant (Tirhakah, King of Ethiopia) had done for Israel; he was doing what Ham's descendants (Egyptian Africans) had done for the baby Jesus; he was fighting for and assisting God's righteousness.

Note that the bible identifies Simon explicitly as a native of Cyrene, the Libyan city in Africa. Keep in mind that we have previously shown that Libya is the nation that developed from Ham's son Put and is a North African nation even to this day.

Simon of Cyrene was Biblically Black and Blessed!

Ethiopian Eunuch

Acts 8:26-28 reads

> [26] And the angel of the Lord spake unto Philip, saying, Arise, and go toward the south unto the way that goeth down from Jerusalem unto Gaza, which is desert.
>
> [27] And he arose and went: and, behold, **a man of Ethiopia**, an eunuch of great authority under Candace queen of the Ethiopians, who had the charge of all her treasure, and had come to Jerusalem for to worship,
>
> [28] Was returning, and sitting in his chariot read Esaias the prophet.

In these verses, two prominent descendants of Ham are identified.

First, there is the Ethiopian Eunuch, who the Bible identifies as Queen Candace's treasurer, and as such, he has great authority under her rule. When God instructed Phillip to approach him, he was sitting in his chariot reading God's word, seeking more in-depth knowledge of God. This speaks volumes about him, but in a greater sense, it validates and verifies the commitment and relationship that black people have with God. I will also say this; with this incident, we get a clear snapshot of the calling of Israel. As earlier stated in this book, Israel's call as God's priests, relative to the descendants of Ham, was to make God known unto them so that they would have knowledge of the God who they WERE ALREADY serving. THIS IS EXACTLY WHAT PHILLIP DID!

The second prominent descendant of Ham identified here is Queen Candace of Ethiopia. She was in a position of authority, power, and wealth. No further knowledge of her is required to establish that she enjoyed the favor of the omnipotent God that she served.

Both the Ethiopian Eunuch and Ethiopian Queen were Biblically Black and Blessed!

Solomon's Black Love

Song of Solomon 1:5 reads

> [5] I am black, but comely, O ye daughters of Jerusalem, as the tents of Kedar, as the curtains of Solomon.

The bible does not provide much information about this particular woman except that she was black, beautiful, or comely, and Solomon loved her. Once again, the beauty of black women is emphasized by scripture! Wives and lovers of leaders possess enormous influence with the leader, and therefore power.

We could go into detail about the 'tents of Kedar', but I will suffice it to say that they were desirable above other tents, so this speaks of the enormous desire one would have for a person of such beauty.

Solomon's Black Love was Biblically Black and Blessed!

I have referenced only a few of Ham's descendants as they are presented in the bible. Keep in mind that there will be inherently more Jewish people mentioned in the bible than other ethnic groups simply because of their function as Priests. They are responsible for sharing God's word and instructions with the world.

Since it is Israel's God-given mission first to acquire knowledge of God and share it, as well as handle God's word as priests, it is understandable that the bible would contain more information about them because it follows them as they receive the word from the sender (God) and deliver the word to the receiver (all the world). That makes Israel the delivery mechanism. But when Israel was confronted with destructive opposition from those that opposed God, God would send them to His people in Africa for protection or send His people from Africa up to protect them. We see God's assignment to black people most times that Israel was threatened or in trouble.

Black People Restored

"*P*rinces shall come out of Egypt; Ethiopia shall soon stretch out her hands unto God."[xliv]

We have seen in this book that both Adam and Eve were black. We also have seen that after the flood, the entire world proceeded from Noah's sons. Since Ham's descendants remained in the land near the equator, they retained the original skin color of Adam and Eve.

Furthermore, we showed that black people are the descendants of Ham, and God has always had a very special relationship with Ham's descendants. Ham's descendants were in a relationship with God before Abraham was called from his father's house. Historically, they have served as the protectors of God's righteousness, and black people are very prominent in God's plan for this world.

Black people were, and always will be, God's people of Power, Strength, and Wealth! Black people are royal people of focus that have been set apart by God. So what has happened to so many of Ham's descendants today?

As long as Ham's seed was serving and worshipping God, they were in unison with God, even when they served God without direct knowledge of who He was. And God responded to their commitment and dedication by blessing them abundantly above other nations. Health, riches, wealth, peace, and many God given blessings were placed in their possession. These blessings were given to them in the very sacred ground that God deeded to them. But then the land became contaminated through a process called colonization!

When we consider God's assignment to Shem's seed, the Jews, we see that they have failed miserably to fulfill their mission and are not completing that assignment as a nation even today. As we previously stated, their assignment was to receive knowledge of God, share that knowledge with Ham's seed so that they would no longer 'ignorantly' worship God, and bring Japheth's seed, the Gentiles, back into relationship with God. The Jews failure was so great that God sent Jesus to re-focus them on the work He initially selected them for. God sent Jesus through Abraham's seed to fulfill His initial assignment to Israel through Jesus. When Shem's seed failed to function as priests to the world and bring the seed of Japheth back into a relationship with God, Japheth's descendants forcefully and violently enlarged themselves. Colonization was the process through which Japheth's descendants forcefully and violently exerted control over much of the land that God gave specifically to Ham and his descendants. With an eye on the precious goods and valuable natural resources of the land, Japheth's descendants wreaked havoc upon the land, its people, and its resources. The natural resources were taken to enrich those whom God had not blessed with such valuable resources, and the countries were forced into submission. Not only were the precious natural resources taken, but the people were forcibly taken from the country and enslaved. Then the perpetrators of this great injustice against the African people and people of African descent presented Africa and Africans to the world as poor, uneducated savages that worshipped idol Gods. They misled the world with their presentation of Africa and its people. This misleading was done to maintain control over the indigenous Africans and reinforce discrimination against black people globally. Even today, conditions such as low socioeconomic status, social deprivation, inadequate education, high unemployment, and the criminal industrial complex are systematically implemented against black people to reinforce this negative mentality. These inequalities and injustices yet impact and negatively affect behavior in the Black community today.

But this was not the will of God. It is not in the character or make-up of black people to be enslaved, controlled, dominated, and abused by any other race or ethnic group. The enslavement and forced servitude of black people have always led to violence. It will always create violent tension among the inhabitants of the world simply because black people cannot and will not live peaceably in forced servitude, slavery, discrimination, prejudice, etc. As long as Ham's descendants have injustice forcefully thrust upon them, peace cannot prevail in the world! As long as the unrighteous exploitation of black people, their God given land, their talents, and resources continues, there will be no earthly peace because of the nature of God's relationship with Black People! God created Black people to be His emissaries of strength, the strong protectors of His righteousness. This strength can never be bridled for unrighteousness, **AND ONLY GOD CAN EXERT CONTROL OVER HIS PEOPLE OF STRENGTH!**

Black people also yearn for a spiritual relationship with the God of their ancestors, the God of Ham, the true and living God! This explains the spiritual nature inherent within black people and our desire to worship today! And although one may make the argument that Canaan was cursed, as previously shown, it was never God's plan for Ethiopia (Black People), Mizraim (Egypt), or Put (Libya) to endure the harshness of discrimination, prejudice, racism, or servitude of any type.

God's assignment to Ham's descendants remains intact because God will never repent for selecting them for this function. Africa and its people will rise! Africa and its people will be restored! Indeed, Princes will proceed from Egypt, and Ethiopia (Black People) will lift their hands to God with knowledge. Even as I write this book, we are witnessing indigenous black people everywhere rise and demonstrate the blessings and favor of God upon their lives. We are seeing the shifting of control in many African nations back into the hands of the indigenous African inhabitants. We are also seeing the elevation of African descendants to positions that were not available or even accessible to them in the past. This will only continue as Ham's descendants return to their rightful biblical place of Power, Strength, and Wealth.

We will see a renewed relationship between Black people and Jewish people. Just as Israel continually went to Africa in biblical times and Africa responded positively, with the exception of the Egyptian Pharaoh that God raised to enslave the Jewish people, God's plan has always had these two groups of people functioning together in divine harmony.

Black people are God's people, and we are blessed when we acknowledge our God, accept His assignment to us, and live-in obedience and submission to Him, AND ONLY TO HIM!

According to scripture, black people, or the descendants of Ham, are……

Biblically Black and Blessed!

References & Credits

i Genesis 1:KJV
ii https://www.merriam-webster.com/dictionary/beginning
iii Revelation 1:8 KJV; Revelation 22:13 KJV
iv Genesis 1:31 KJV
v Genesis 2:10-14 KJV
vi Revelation 12:9 KJV
vii Colossians 1:16 KJV
viii T. Luke 10:18
ix Job 1:6 KJV; Revelation 12:10 KJV
x Wayne Jackson '**Who is Lucifer**'
xi Ezekiel 28:18 KJV
xii US Geological Survey (https://pubs.usgs.gov/gip/geotime/age.html)
xiii Smithsonian National Museum of Natural History (http://humanorigins.si.edu/education/introduction-human-evolution)
xiv 1 Thessalonians 5:23 KJV
xv Genesis 1:27 KJV
xvi Genesis 2:7 KJV
xvii Hebrews 2:6-7
xviii Job 40:15
xix Genesis 1:28 KJV
xx Genesis 2:8 KJV
xxi Daniel 10:4 KJV
xxii *Liddell, Henry George; Scott, Robert, A Greek-English Lexicon*
xxiii Genesis 2:23 KJV
xxiv Newsweek 1988 '**The Search For Adam and Eve**' (http://www.virginia.edu/woodson/courses/aas102%20(spring%2001)/articles/tierney.html)

xxv Science Magazine June 2017 '**World's oldest Homo sapiens fossils found in Morocco**'
https://www.sciencemag.org/news/2017/06/world-s-oldest-homo-sapiens-fossils-found-morocco
xxvi Genesis 6:5-6 KJV
xxvii Genesis 9:18-19 KJV

[xxviii] Nina Jablonski "***Understanding Race The American Anthropological Society***"
http://www.understandingrace.com/humvar/skin_01.html
[xxix] Jeremiah 31:29-33 KJV; Ezekiel 18:20-24 KJV
[xxx] Romans 10:12 KJV
[xxxi] Amos 9:7 KJV
[xxxii] 1 Corinthians 12:29 KJV
[xxxiii] 1 Corinthians 12:29 KJV
[xxxiv] Deuteronomy 18:1-5 KJV
[xxxv] Luke 1:11-28 KJV; Daniel 9:21-27 KJV;
[xxxvi] Daniel 12:1 KJV; Revelation 12:7-9 KJV; Jude 1:9 KJV
[xxxvii] Exodus 3:13-14 KJV
[xxxviii] Romans 9:17 KJV
[xxxix] Romans 11:29 KJV
[xl] Jeremiah 13:23 KJV
[xli] Matthew 12:42 KJV
[xlii] Amos 9:7 KJV
[xliii] blacksin the bible.org
[xliv] Psalms 68:31 KJV

www.ingramcontent.com/pod-product-compliance
Lightning Source LLC
Chambersburg PA
CBHW041215070526
44579CB00001B/1